POCKET **ROUGH GUIDE**
EDINBURGH

Written and researched by
BRENDON GRIFFIN AND KEITH MUNRO

CONTENTS

EDINBURGH

Venerable, dramatic Edinburgh, the showcase capital of Scotland, is a historic, cultured and cosmopolitan city, regularly topping polls as the most desirable place to live in the United Kingdom. Of course, the locals have always known as much, savouring a skyline built on a series of extinct volcanoes and rocky crags which rise from the generally flat landscape of the Lothians, with the sheltered shoreline of the Firth of Forth to the north. "My own Romantic town", Sir Walter Scott called it, although it was another Edinburgh-born author, Robert Louis Stevenson, who perhaps best captured the feel of his "precipitous city", declaring that "No situation could be more commanding for the head of a kingdom; none better chosen for noble prospects."

View of Holyroodhouse Palace and Calton Hill

Along with its beauty, Edinburgh is blessed by its brevity, a wonderfully compact city built for navigation on foot. The centre has two distinct parts: the unrelentingly medieval Old Town, with its tortuous alleys and tightly packed closes, and the dignified, eighteenth-century Grecian-style New Town. Dividing the two are Princes Street Gardens, which run roughly east to west under the shadow of Edinburgh Castle. Set on the hill that rolls down from the fairy tale Castle to the royal Palace of Holyroodhouse, the Old Town preserves all the key landmarks from its role as a historic capital, augmented by the dramatic and unusual Scottish Parliament building, opposite the palace, and the attendant redevelopment of both Holyrood Road and the area around Market Street and New Street just off the Royal Mile. A few hundred yards away, a tantalizing glimpse of wild Scotland can be had in Holyrood Park, an extensive and unique area of real live wilderness bang in the centre of the city, dominated by Arthur's Seat, the largest and most impressive of the city's volcanoes.

Among Edinburgh's many museums, the exciting National Museum of Scotland houses ten thousand of Scotland's most precious artefacts, while the National Gallery of Scotland and its offshoot, the Scottish National Gallery of Modern Art, have two of Britain's finest collections of paintings.

Award-winning vegan food at Harmonium Leith

In August, around a million visitors flock to the city for the Edinburgh Festival, in fact a series of separate festivals that make up the largest arts extravaganza in the world. On a less elevated theme, the city's vast array of distinctive pubs, allied to its brewing and distilling traditions, make it an unrivalled drinking city. Its four universities, plus several colleges, mean that there is a youthful presence for most of the year. The Summerhall arts complex (see page 119) is Edinburgh's biggest arts venue, while the Cowgate hosts many of the city's best club nights.

What's new

With everyone from Beyoncé to Brad Pitt and even Jeremy Corbyn giving the once stigmatised world of veganism a glamorous name, Edinburgh has stepped up to the animal-free plate with an ever-growing number of cafés, restaurants and pubs catering to clean, conscience-salving eating. Even committed carnivores have been known to drool over the recently opened *Harmonium* (see page 103) while the brilliantly named *Holy Cow* (see page 83) has the city abuzz with their jackfruit burgers, the gorgeous creations at *Pumpkin Brown* (see page 53) remain much-Instagrammed things of beauty, and *Paradise Palms* (see page 55) are stylishly giving it the vegan "V".

The ruins of Tantallon Castle, East Lothian

With a number of bars (several with live music) open till 3am year-round, there's always a heaving dancefloor somewhere in the city.

Beyond the city centre, the liveliest area is Leith, the city's medieval port, a culinary quartier developing at lightning speed, with a heady, beardy mix of traditional and cutting-edge bars, upmarket seafood restaurants and seasonal foragers.

The wider rural hinterland of Edinburgh, known as the Lothians, mixes rolling countryside and attractive country towns with some impressive historic ruins. In East Lothian, blustery clifftop paths lead to the romantic battlements of Tantallon Castle, while the most famous sight in Midlothian is the mysterious fifteenth-century Rosslyn Chapel. To the northwest of the city, both the dramatic steel geometry of the Forth Rail Bridge and the graceful towers of the recently completed Queensferry Crossing (the longest bridge of its kind in the world) are best viewed by walking across the Forth Road bridge, starting at South Queensferry.

When to visit

Being closer to sunny East Lothian than the sodden west coast, Edinburgh's main climatic drawback is not so much precipitation as biting wind. Even in summer, sea breezes can keep temperatures down, as can the *haar*, mist that sometimes rolls in after a spell of fine weather. In recent years, March, April and May have seen some of the best and most prolonged spells of warm sunshine and blue skies (enhanced, in May at least, by wonderfully long days and short nights). The summer months of June, July and especially August (average max 17–19°) are notoriously unpredictable and often wet, as Fringe regulars know only too well. While winters are generally cold (average max 7–10°) and gloomy, you can still be lucky and hit upon a gorgeous few days of crisp sunshine. Crowds of tourists now throng Edinburgh year-round, reaching a peak during the Fringe, Christmas and especially New Year.

Where to...

Shop

While Edinburgh has traditionally been outdone on the designer clothing front by Glasgow, Multrees Walk and its **Harvey Nichols** store goes someway to redressing the balance. If labels are your thing, you'll find enough here and in nearby George Street to blow your entire travel budget in a couple of hours. For vintage gear, independent designers, comics, antiquarian books and even fossils, the Old Town is your oyster, especially Candlemaker Row, Victoria Street, the Grassmarket and West Port. Stockbridge (especially St Stephen Street) and Newington are also good bets for quirky boutiques and antique shops. For delis and artisan food shopping, again the Old Town and Stockbridge come up trumps, as does Marchmont, Bruntsfield and Morningside.
OUR FAVOURITES: Diagon House see page 52. W. Armstrong see page 52. Mr Wood's Fossils see page 52.

Eat

As you'd expect for a capital city, Edinburgh's exceptionally dynamic eating scene offers Scotland's most comprehensive dining, with everything from cheapie cosmopolitan pies to fresh-from-the-quayside seafood to hipster pop-up and seasonally-foraged heaven and a kaleidoscopic array of ethnic eats, with plenty of Michelin stars to go round. Lunch is usually served between noon and 2pm, when you can dine on a gourmet quality, two or even three-course meal for around £10 to £15. In the evening, restaurants start filling up from around 7pm and serve till 10/11pm. The sheer weight of Edinburgh's tourist numbers, however, means that many places serve food round the clock, seven days a week, and are packed round the clock; don't ever assume you can simply turn up and get a table. Generally, the Old Town remains the locus of traditional, pricey Scottish and French-influenced cuisine, ever more locally sourced, while Leith, naturally, is home to the most renowned seafood, and, increasingly, the most exciting and creative new ventures.
OUR FAVOURITES: Dishoom see page 83. Harmonium see page 103. Tupiniquim see page 9.

Drink

Edinburgh is a drinker's shangri-la, with almost every variety of alcoholic beverage available, and a bewildering array of premises to serve them in. In a turn of events harking back to the dim and distant past when some Scottish villages had more breweries than churches, the stuff is increasingly being concocted at micro level within the city itself rather than shipped in, with artisan distillers and brewers popping up on every other street corner. Very generally speaking, the Old Town is your best bet for a traditional Scottish pub; Newington is studded with boisterous student bars; the West End, Stockbridge and New Town specialize in wine bars and quirky one-offs, while Leith and Portobello are hipster central. Edinburgh licensing laws are gloriously liberal, at least for the UK, with most places open till at least 1am and some till 3am.
OUR FAVOURITES: Royal Dick see page 119. Café Royal Circle Bar see page 75. Teuchters Landing see page 105.

The Main Ingredient: Al Fresco Edinburgh

Whether you're a fully blogged-up gastronome, Instagram-happy snapper or just someone who likes your food, be assured that Edinburgh is second only to London in the UK's culinary pecking order, and the oft-satirised old chestnut about having "had your tea" outlived its sell-by date decades ago. On the contrary, you may well never get enough of your tea [as in dinner] in this city, so comprehensive, creative and ever-expanding is the range of food and drink on offer, and so committed are an increasing number of chefs and restaurateurs to quality native produce and local, ethical sourcing. The drive towards everything artisan, organic, seasonal, foraged and local has inevitably gone hand in hand with a flowering of farmers' markets, street food, kiosks, pop-ups and festivals. We've listed the most prominent examples below but the dynamism of the Edinburgh scene means that the best experiences can often be the most spontaneous and unexpected, especially during the Fringe when all manner of wild and wonderful pop-ups bloom for a few short weeks: keep your eyes peeled and your nose trained.

EDINBURGH FARMERS' MARKET
MAP P.88, POCKET MAP D5

Castle Terrace ☎ 0131 220 8580, Ⓦ edinburghfarmersmarket.co.uk. Sat 9am–2pm.
The trademark blue-and-white striped awnings are host to everything you'd expect from such a veteran player: hand-made cheese, organic charcuterie, grass-fed meat, seasonal organic veg, award-winning fruit wines and more, plus demos by Edinburgh Slow Food.

EDINBURGH FOOD FESTIVAL
MAP P.116, POCKET MAP E6

George Square, Newington ☎ 0131 623 3030, Ⓦ edfoodfest.com. Late July.
The benches of lovely George Square Gardens are warmed up in late July with this pre-Fringe affair run by Assembly (see page 149). Aiming to stimulate grey matter as well as taste buds, with plenty of expert Scottish foodie debate, entertainment and demos alongside the specialist comestibles. Free.

FOODIES FESTIVAL
MAP P.94, POCKET MAP B2

Inverleith Park Ⓦ foodiesfestival.com. Early August.
Wielding a list of corporate sponsors as long as a string of aged garlic and an all-star line-up of Michelin star-holding chefs and Masterchef and Great British Bake Off winners, this UK-touring festival pitches up in sunny Inverleith in early August for three days of interactive cooking,

masterclasses and over-consumption. The 2017 bash featured beer critic Melissa Cole bravely attempting to "take the beard out of beer". About time someone did. Day tickets £14; three-day ticket £20.

THE FOOD N' FLEA
MAP P.30, POCKET MAP E14

New St ☎ 07736 281 893, Ⓦ thepitt.co.uk/foodnflea. Daily 11am–5pm.

Conceived by the folk behind The Pitt (see below), this is Edinburgh's first permanent daily street food market, taking the taste to the heart of Edinburgh's Old Town with a monthly rotation of vendors selling delicacies like wood fired pizzas and Kenyan curries. An array of local designers, makers and vintage traders comprise the "Flea".

GRASSMARKET MARKET
MAP P.48, POCKET MAP B16
Central Reservation, Grassmarket ☏ 0131 261 6181, ⓦ stockbridgemarket.com/grassmarket.html. Sat 10am–5pm.
Thriving little market with predominately artisan food sellers offering things like bread, cheese, olives and fresh veg as well as delicious cooked meals such as paella.

LEITH MARKET
MAP P.100, POCKET MAP B11
Dock Place, Leith ☏ 0131 261 6181, ⓦ stockbridgemarket.com/leith.html. Sat 10am–5pm.
Another satellite of Stockbridge Market, with a similar line-up of fairtrade, organic and ethnic eats. Perfect for an after-market pint in the beer garden at nearby *Teuchters Landing* (see page 105).

MILK AT COLLECTIVE
MAP P.68, POCKET MAP E13
City Observatory & City Dome, Calton Hill ☏ 0131 556 1264, ⓦ cafemilk.co.uk/calton-hill. Daily 10am–5pm.
For years the best you could hope for lunch on Calton Hill was a stale sandwich from a local newsagent. No longer. Attached to the temporary Collective Gallery site, this DIY kiosk serves delicious seasonal and locally sourced snacks.

THE PITT
MAP P.100, POCKET MAP A12
125 Pitt St, Leith ☏ 07736 281 893, ⓦ thepitt.co.uk. Sat noon–10pm.
This weekly aggregate of vendors remains the beating industrial heart of Edinburgh's street food scene, serving out of gritty premises on an unglamorous Leith backstreet, with craft beer, live music and a festive vibe packing in the locals like artisan sardines. £2 entry fee.

STOCKBRIDGE MARKET
MAP P.94, POCKET MAP C3
Kerr St, Stockbridge ☏ 0131 261 6181, ⓦ stockbridgemarket.com. Sun 10am–5pm.
A compact affair under a grove of leaning Sorbus trees by the banks of the Water of Leith. Even with the belligerent Scottish climate, there's somehow an international buzz as scores of locals and tourists dine out on paella or Bombay street food, or wash a cupcake down with a coffee served out of the back of a VW camper.

TUPINIQUIM
MAP P.48, POCKET MAP D6
Top of Middle Meadow Walk, Lauriston Place, Old Town ☏ 0790 886 184, ⓦ tupiniquim.co.uk. Daily 10am–6pm.
Edinburgh's best loved food kiosk, this old police box turned funky Brazilian creperie has many a loyal lunchtime customer. The legendary, gluten-free crepes come in both sweet and savoury varieties, filled with everything from steak to pumpkin to guava jam, and served with a personal touch that could only hail from Brazil.

Edinburgh at a glance

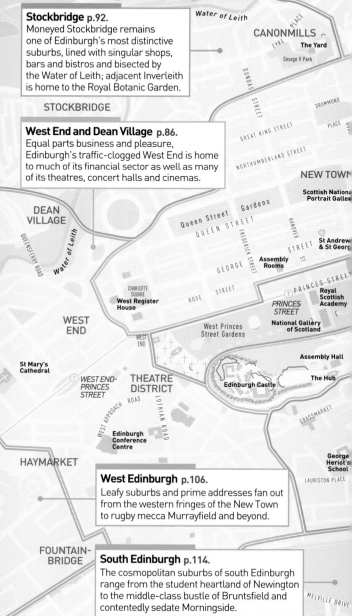

Stockbridge p.92.
Moneyed Stockbridge remains one of Edinburgh's most distinctive suburbs, lined with singular shops, bars and bistros and bisected by the Water of Leith; adjacent Inverleith is home to the Royal Botanic Garden.

West End and Dean Village p.86.
Equal parts business and pleasure, Edinburgh's traffic-clogged West End is home to much of its financial sector as well as many of its theatres, concert halls and cinemas.

West Edinburgh p.106.
Leafy suburbs and prime addresses fan out from the western fringes of the New Town to rugby mecca Murrayfield and beyond.

South Edinburgh p.114.
The cosmopolitan suburbs of south Edinburgh range from the student heartland of Newington to the middle-class bustle of Bruntsfield and contentedly sedate Morningside.

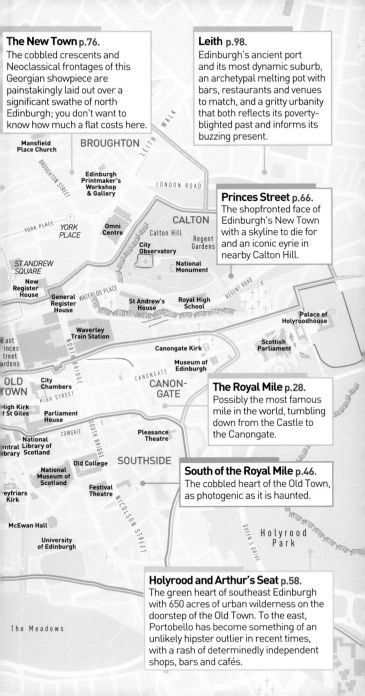

The New Town p.76.
The cobbled crescents and Neoclassical frontages of this Georgian showpiece are painstakingly laid out over a significant swathe of north Edinburgh; you don't want to know how much a flat costs here.

Leith p.98.
Edinburgh's ancient port and its most dynamic suburb, an archetypal melting pot with bars, restaurants and venues to match, and a gritty urbanity that both reflects its poverty-blighted past and informs its buzzing present.

Princes Street p.66.
The shopfronted face of Edinburgh's New Town with a skyline to die for and an iconic eyrie in nearby Calton Hill.

The Royal Mile p.28.
Possibly the most famous mile in the world, tumbling down from the Castle to the Canongate.

South of the Royal Mile p.46.
The cobbled heart of the Old Town, as photogenic as it is haunted.

Holyrood and Arthur's Seat p.58.
The green heart of southeast Edinburgh with 650 acres of urban wilderness on the doorstep of the Old Town. To the east, Portobello has become something of an unlikely hipster outlier in recent times, with a rash of determinedly independent shops, bars and cafés.

Mansfield Place Church
BROUGHTON
BROUGHTON STREET
LEITH WALK
Edinburgh Printmaker's Workshop & Gallery
LONDON ROAD
YORK PLACE
YORK PLACE
Omni Centre
CALTON
Calton Hill
Regent Gardens
City Observatory
ST ANDREW SQUARE
New Register House
National Monument
General Register House
WATERLOO PLACE
St Andrew's House
Royal High School
REGENT ROAD
East Princes Street Gardens
Waverley Train Station
NORTH BRIDGE
Canongate Kirk
Palace of Holyroodhouse
Scottish Parliament
OLD TOWN
City Chambers
HIGH STREET
Museum of Edinburgh
CANONGATE
CANON-GATE
High Kirk of St Giles
Parliament House
COWGATE
SOUTH BRIDGE
Pleasance Theatre
National Library of Scotland
Central Library
Old College
SOUTHSIDE
National Museum of Scotland
Festival Theatre
Greyfriars Kirk
NICOLSON STREET
McEwan Hall
University of Edinburgh
QUEEN'S DRIVE
Holyrood Park
The Meadows

14 Things not to miss

It's not possible to see everything that Edinburgh has to offer in one trip – and we don't suggest you try. What follows is a selective taste of the city's highlights, from its world famous architecture to its August arts festivities.

> **The Palace of Holyroodhouse**

See page 58

For centuries the sometime residence of Scotland's kings and queens, with a hauntingly ruinous abbey.

< **Edinburgh Castle**

See page 28

Possibly the most iconic castle on earth, home to one of the world's most celebrated military parades.

∨ **The Scottish Parliament**

See page 59

An architectural one-off that still divides opinion; squeeze in among the tourist hordes and decide for yourself.

‹ Dr Neil's Garden
See page 63
Get even further off the beaten track in this low-key idyll by Duddingston Village.

⌄ The Old Town
See page 46
The haunted heart of old Edinburgh, with tenements, closes and catacombs piled up cheek-by-jowl.

City skyline
See page 71
The classic sightline southwest from Calton Hill, taking in the Old Town in all its brooding magnificence.

Rosslyn Chapel
See page 125
Da Vinci Code fever may have cooled but this gothic masterpiece is as mesmerising as ever.

∧ **The Edinburgh Festival**
See page 148
The whole world descends on Edinburgh come August for the mother of all arts extravaganzas.

∨ **The New Town**
See page 76
The Old Town's polar opposite, with dazzling Georgian crescents, postcard-pretty mews and manicured gardens.

∧ The Shore
See page 99
Leith's medieval port and surrounds are a foodie paradise of Michelin stars, foraged produce and ethnic eats.

< Royal Botanic Garden
See page 94
Edinburgh's showpiece gardens, with the world's biggest collection of wild Asian plants outside China.

∨ **Edinburgh's pubs**
See page 7
From Scotland's oldest pub to craft beer emporia to artisan gin palaces, Edinburgh is a drinker's paradise.

Day One

The Scottish Parliament. See page 59. Get close up with Scotland's most talked about building and – if the parliament is in session – witness devolved government in action.

Palace of Holyroodhouse. See page 58. The former home of Scotland's Stewart kings and queens, with an atmospheric abbey ruin out back.

The Royal Mile. See page 28. Stroll for one full Scots mile along a thoroughfare Daniel Defoe described as "the largest, longest and finest...in the world".

Victoria Street. See page 46. Take a side-trip down selfie-friendly Victoria Street, with its arcaded boutiques and vertigo-inducing pedestrian walkway.

Shopping on Victoria Street

Lunch. See page 41. Drop in to the dazzling Signet Library on the Royal Mile's Parliament Square for the most well-appointed of lunches.

Edinburgh Castle. See page 28. Castles don't come much more legendary than Edinburgh's, or as formidable; even Bonnie Prince Charlie couldn't breach it.

National Gallery of Scotland. See page 70. Make your way down the Mound to Scotland's most comprehensive collection of pre-twentieth-century art.

Colonnades at the Signet Library

Princes Street Gardens. See page 69. Wander among squirrels, flower beds and mature trees in the magnificent shadow of the Edinburgh skyline.

Dinner. See page 83. Head along Princes Street to St Andrew Square for a delicious Indo-Persian meal at buzzing *Dishoom*.

Princes Street Gardens

Day Two

Dynamic Earth. See page 61. The fearsome power of mother nature explained in family-friendly techno-detail.

National Museum of Scotland. See page 51. All the Scottish history you could want; the recent Bonnie Prince Charlie and the Jacobites exhibition generated extensive media coverage.

Greyfriars Kirk. See page 48. Scotland's most famous church, guarded by Scotland's most famous "dug"; just don't rub his nose!

The Grassmarket. See page 46. Wind your way down Candlemaker Row to the historic Grassmarket, once a cattle mart, now a cobbled, al fresco drinking spot, perfect for an aperitif.

 Lunch. See page 9. Nip across to Middle Meadow Walk for a lunch-on-the-hoof at *Tupiniquim*, one of the city's most endearing street food kiosks.

Bruntsfield. See page 115. Explore the boutiques, bistros and artisan cafés of this fashionable enclave.

Dinner. See page 118. Hobnob with the locals at the pillar of Bruntsfield's eating and drinking establishment, *Montpeliers*.

The Dominion Cinema. See page 115. Admire the unusual Art Deco exterior, then ease back into one of the most luxurious film experiences in Scotland.

Dynamic Earth

Boutiques in Bruntsfield

The Art Deco Dominion cinema

Day Three

Calton Hill. See page 71. The best vantage point in the city, according to Robert Louis Stevenson, and he knew a good view when he saw one.

Scottish National Portrait Gallery. See page 78. The story of Scotland in famous physiognomy, with tens of thousands of portraits housed in a dramatic Gothic Revival pile.

The New Town. See page 76. Marvel at the Neoclassical neatness of Edinburgh's eighteenth-century showpiece and lose yourself amid its cobbled mews, gardens and terraces.

Stockbridge. See page 92. Explore the cafés, bars and shops of this singular and perennially hip New Town satellite by the Water of Leith.

Lunch. See page 97. Splash out at celebrity chef Tom Kitchin's gastro-pub, *The Scran & Scallie.*

Royal Botanic Garden. See page 94. Seventy acres of gorgeous garden, famous for its horticultural chinoiserie and handsome glasshouses.

Leith. See page 98. Wander down the Water of Leith walkways to Leith itself, an incredibly dynamic melting pot of michelin-starred restaurants, hipster foodie ventures and reclaimed arts hubs.

Dinner. See page 104. Get into the Leith spirit with four courses of painstakingly handcrafted, fermented and foraged food at the much-heralded *Norn.*

Georgian housing in The New Town

Artisan food shop in Stockbridge

Scottish fine dining at Norn

Green Edinburgh

Even the most full-on city break needs some downtime; recover your calm among Edinburgh's glorious green acres.

Holyrood Park. See page 62. A wonderland of an urban refuge, with no less than 650 acres of hills, glens, lochs and trails.

Arthur's Seat. See page 62. You can't say you've visited Edinburgh if you haven't climbed this iconic volcano; just don't expect any knights or round tables.

Dr Neil's Garden. See page 63. An urban refuge within an urban refuge; feel the stress melting away as you sink onto a stone bench with Duddingston Loch-side views.

Lunch. See page 65. Follow in the footsteps of Stewart – *and* Hanoverian – royalty at Scotland's oldest pub, *The Sheep Heid*.

Meadows. See page 114. Wander the tree-lined walkways of this iconic park and – if it's sunny – picnic with the locals.

Blackford Hill. See page 116. A gentler climb than Arthur's Seat, and home to the Royal Observatory.

Hermitage of Braid. See page 116. Head straight from Blackford Hill into this ancient woodland-designated nature reserve with some of the city's most venerable old trees.

Pentland Hills. See page 125. If you have any energy left, take a bus out to the Pentland Hills for a bracing taste of rural Scottish upland.

Dinner. See page 119. Gird yourself for drinks and dinner in the living museum that is Morningside's *Canny Man*.

Arthur's Seat

The Sheep Heid

Blackford Hill

Infamous Edinburgh

Dastardly deeds; gruesome exhibits; ghosts with a chip on their ectoplasmic shoulder – you'll find it all in the world's most haunted city.

James V's Tower, Palace of Holyroodhouse. See page 58. Scene of the murder of Mary Queen of Scots' secretary, David Rizzio, with the blood stains supposedly still visible.

Surgeon's Hall Museum. See page 51. A conspicuously ostentatious exterior hiding one of Scotland's grisliest museum collections.

The Real Mary King's Close. See page 35. Dodge the ghosts in this dank warren of subterranean tenements, where plague victims were once entombed alive.

Lunch. See page 42. If your appetite hasn't deserted you, head to *Deacon's House Café*, in the haunted close where the man who infamously inspired *Dr Jekyll and Mr Hyde* (see page 34) once lived.

Damnation Alley, South Bridge Vaults. See page 45. Home to a particularly unpleasant poltergeist, these notoriously creepy catacombs consistently take the honours as Edinburgh's most haunted.

Edinburgh Castle. See page 28. The Witches Well, or Fountain, marks the site where hundreds of women were burnt at the stake, while a disembodied piper, Gallic phantoms and a headless drummer are all reported to stalk the castle corridors.

Dinner. See page 44. Where else to dine after a hard day's ghost hunting but amid the Gothic splendour of *The Witchery by the Castle*.

Greyfriars Kirkyard. See page 48. Run the gauntlet of the downright dangerous McKenzie Poltergeist on a night-time tour into the depths of the Covenanter's Prison and Black Mausoleum; sceptics be warned, you'll need nerves of steel.

Surgeon's Hall Museum

Deacon's House Café

Greyfriars Kirkyard

Budget Edinburgh

If you're counting your pounds and pence, it's entirely possible to enjoy an absorbing day's sightseeing completely gratis, and eat for a fraction of the typically prohibitive price.

Ingleby Gallery. See page 73. Tucked away on handsome Carlton Terrace, this is one of Scotland's most prestigious private art galleries.

Old Calton Burial Ground. See page 72. This atmospheric tangle of stones is home to many of Edinburgh's great and good, including David Hume.

Scottish Poetry Library. See page 40. Everyone knows Rabbie Burns but here you'll discover a whole universe of native verse, including recordings in both Scots and Gaelic.

Museum of Edinburgh. See page 37. If you've been on the white-knuckle ghost tour of Greyfriars Kirkyard (see page 24), you might want to fill in some background in this maze of wood-panelled rooms, one of which displays the original National Covenant.

Scottish Poetry Library

Lunch. See page 64. Save money and give something back at the same time in the volunteer-run *Serenity Café*, where all profits are ploughed back into helping others.

Art exhibition at the Talbot Rice Gallery

Old College and Talbot Rice Gallery. See page 51. Contemporary and nineteenth-century art amid the elegant environs of the Robert Adam/William Playfair-designed Old College.

Dean Village. See page 87. It's a bit of a hike out past the West End but chocolate box-pretty Dean Village has an atmosphere all of its own.

Scottish National Gallery of Modern Art. See page 89. Britain's first gallery dedicated to twentieth-century painting and sculpture, with a strong showing by the Scottish Colourists and a career's worth of genius by Leith's own Pop Art godfather, Eduardo Paolozzi.

Dean Village

PLACES

Royal Mile

The Royal Mile

The Royal Mile's tight, foreboding closes dwarfed by soaring rubble-stone merchant houses and grand neo-Grecian sandstone buildings make it a veritable feast of architectural heritage. Scratch the surface and it gets even more interesting as many of the structures here sit atop a medieval subterranean world of caverns, rooms and closes, some of which can be visited on tours while others are yet to be rediscovered. Comprising four separate streets in a row (Castlehill, Lawnmarket, High Street and Canongate) and bookended by the Castle and the Palace of Holyroodhouse, the Royal Mile possesses an enviable number of sights and attractions only exceeded (and somewhat detracted) by the inexhaustible knitwear, tartan and shortbread outlets that, along with the ever-present bagpiper, draw tourists here in their droves.

Edinburgh Castle

MAP P.29, POCKET MAP A15
Castlehill ☎ 0131 225 9846,
ⓦ edinburghcastle.gov.uk. Daily:
April–Sept 9.30am–6pm; Oct–March
9.30am–5pm (last entry 1hr before
closing); guided tours (every 15min–1hr;
30min) free. Audio tours £3.50 if bought
as part of the entrance fee (pick up near
Portcullis Gate). £17; HES.

The history of Edinburgh is tightly wrapped up with its **Castle**, which

Edinburgh Castle

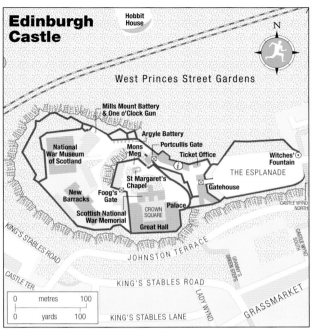

Edinburgh Castle

Hobbit House

West Princes Street Gardens

Mills Mount Battery & One o'Clock Gun

Argyle Battery

National War Museum of Scotland

Mons Meg

Portcullis Gate

Ticket Office

Witches' Fountain

THE ESPLANADE

St Margaret's Chapel

New Barracks

Foog's Gate

Gatehouse

CASTLE WYND NORTH

Scottish National War Memorial

CROWN SQUARE

Palace

Great Hall

CASTLE WYND SOUTH

KING'S STABLES ROAD

JOHNSTON TERRACE

GRANNY'S GREEN STEPS

CASTLE TER.

KING'S STABLES ROAD

LADY WYND

GRASSMARKET

KING'S STABLES LANE

0	metres	100
0	yards	100

dominates the city from a lofty seat atop an extinct volcanic rock. It requires no great imaginative feat to comprehend the strategic importance that underpinned the Castle's, and hence Edinburgh's, pre-eminence in Scotland. From Princes Street, the north side rears high above an almost sheer rock face; the southern side is equally formidable and the western, where the rock rises in terraces, only marginally less so. Would-be attackers, like modern tourists, were forced to approach the Castle from the narrow ridge to the east – today's Royal Mile. The disparate styles of the fortifications reflect the change in its role from defensive citadel to national monument, and today, as well as attracting more paying visitors than any other sight in Scotland, the Castle is still a military barracks and home to the Honours of Scotland, the nation's crown jewels.

The Esplanade to Mill's Mount

The Castle is entered via the **Esplanade**, a parade ground laid out in the eighteenth century and enclosed by ornamental walls. In the summer huge grandstands are erected for the Edinburgh Military Tattoo (see page 145), which takes place nightly during the Edinburgh Festival. A shameless and spectacular pageant of swinging kilts and massed pipe bands, the tattoo makes full use of its dramatic setting. Various memorials are dotted around the Esplanade, including the pretty Art Nouveau **Witches' Fountain** commemorating the three hundred or more women burnt at this spot on charges of sorcery, the last of whom died in 1722.

Edinburgh Castle has a single entrance, a 10ft-wide opening in the **gatehouse**, one of many Romantic-style additions made in

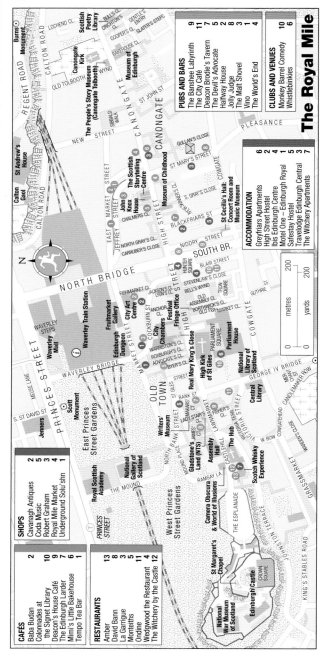

The Royal Mile

CAFÉS

Baba Budan	2
Colonnades at the Signet Library	10
Deacon's House Café	9
The Edinburgh Larder	7
Mimi's Little Bakehouse	6
Tempo Tea Bar	1

RESTAURANTS

Amber	13
David Bann	8
La Garrigue	5
Monteiths	11
Ondine	4
Wedgwood the Restaurant	3
The Witchery by the Castle	12

SHOPS

Cavanagh Antiques	2
Coda Music	5
Robert Graham	3
Royal Mile Market	4
Underground Solu'shn	1

PUBS AND BARS

The Banshee Labyrinth	9
The City Café	11
Deacon Brodie's Tavern	7
The Devil's Advocate	5
Halfway House	2
Jolly Judge	8
The Malt Shovel	3
Vino	1
The World's End	4

CLUBS AND VENUES

Monkey Barrel Comedy	10
Whistlebinkies	6

ACCOMMODATION

Greyfriars Apartments	6
High Street Hostel	2
Ibis Edinburgh Centre	4
Motel One – Edinburgh Royal	1
Safestay Hostel	5
Travelodge Edinburgh Central	3
The Witchery Apartments	7

Crown Square at Edinburgh Castle

the 1880s, through which you'll find the main ticket office on your right. Continue uphill, showing your ticket as you pass through the handsome sixteenth-century **Portcullis Gate**, and you'll soon arrive at the eighteenth-century, six-gun **Argyle Battery**. A few further steps west on **Mill's Mount Battery**, a well-known Edinburgh ritual takes place – the daily firing of the **one o'clock gun**.

National War Museum of Scotland

Entry included in Castle entry fee

Continuing on the main path past the Argyle Battery look out for the **National War Museum of Scotland** on your right. Covering the last four hundred years of Scottish military history, the slant of the museum is towards the soldiers who fought for the Union, rather than against it. While the rooms are packed with uniforms, medals, paintings of heroic actions and plenty of interesting memorabilia, the museum manages to convey a reflective, human tone.

St Margaret's Chapel

Near the highest point of the citadel is tiny Romanesque **St Margaret's Chapel**, the oldest surviving building in the Castle, and probably in Edinburgh. Although once believed to have been built by the saint herself, and mooted as the site of her death in 1093, its architectural style suggests that it actually dates from about thirty years later. In front of the chapel you'll see the famous fifteenth-century siege gun, **Mons Meg**, which could fire a 500lb stone nearly two miles.

Crown Square

The historic heart of the Castle, Crown Square is the most important and secure section of the entire complex. The eastern side is occupied by the **Palace**, a surprisingly unassuming edifice begun in the 1430s, which owes its Renaissance appearance to King James IV. There's access to a few rooms here including the tiny panelled bedchamber where Mary, Queen of Scots gave birth to James VI.

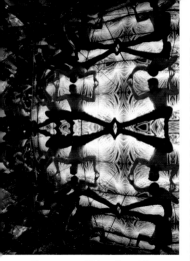
Circus company Elixir perform at Camera Obscura and World of Illusions

The Palace also houses a detailed audio-visual presentation on the **Honours of Scotland**, a potent image of Scotland's nationhood; the originals are housed in the Crown Room at the very end of the display. The glass case containing the Honours has been rearranged to create space for the incongruously plain **Stone of Destiny**, a coronation throne on which all kings of Scotland were crowned from AD838 until Edward I stole it in 1296. The stone was returned ceremoniously from Westminster Abbey in 1996.

On the south side of Crown Square is James IV's hammer beam-ceilinged **Great Hall**, used for meetings of the Scottish Parliament until 1639.

Scotch Whisky Experience

MAP P.30, POCKET MAP B15
354 Castlehill ☎ 0131 220 0441,
Ⓦ scotchwhiskyexperience.co.uk. Daily:
April–Aug 10am–6pm, Sept–March
10am–5pm. Tours from £15.
The **Scotch Whisky Experience** mimics the kind of tours offered at distilleries in the Highlands, and while it can't match the authenticity of the real thing, the centre does

offer a thorough introduction to the "water of life" (*uisge beatha* in Gaelic), with tours featuring an entertaining tutorial on the specialized art of whisky nosing, a gimmicky ride in a moving "barrel" car, a peek at the world's largest whisky collection and a tasting. The Silver tour (50min) is the one to go for if you have a casual interest in the subject or are with children who get in half price. For a deeper understanding of the drink consider a masterclass, which includes a sensory perception test followed by a comparative tasting featuring a blend, a grain and two single malt whiskies. On your way out, a well-stocked shop gives an idea of the sheer range and diversity of the drink, while downstairs there's a pleasant whisky bar and restaurant, *Amber* (see page 43) both of which can be visited without going on a tour.

Camera Obscura and World of Illusions

MAP P.30, POCKET MAP B15
549 Castlehill ☎ 0131 226 3709,
Ⓦ camera-obscura.co.uk. Daily: April–June, Sept & Oct 9.30am–7pm; July & Aug 9.30am–9pm; Nov–March 10am–6pm. £15, children £11, under-5s free.
Edinburgh's **Camera Obscura** has been a tourist attraction since 1853. Housed in the domed black-and-white turret on the roof, the "camera" consists of a small, darkened room with a white wooden table onto which a periscope reflects live images of prominent buildings and folk walking on the streets below. Today, the camera is greatly overshadowed by the **World of Illusions**, a labyrinth of family-friendly exhibits of optical illusions, holograms and clever visual trickery spread across the five floors below the camera. Many are playfully interactive, like the Maze of Mirrors or the Vortex where you attempt to walk across a static ramp surrounded by a rotating tunnel – much harder than you might think. There's also

the Big-Small room where photos taken from the viewing window reveal giant children towering over their shrunken parents.

The Hub

MAP P.30, POCKET MAP B15
348 Castlehill ☎ 0131 473 2000 ⓦ thehub-edinburgh.com. Daily 10am–5pm. Free.
The imposing black church at the foot of Castlehill is **The Hub**, also known as "Edinburgh's Festival Centre". It's open year-round, providing performance, rehearsal and exhibition space, a ticket centre and a café. The building itself was constructed in 1845 to designs by James Gillespie Graham and Augustus Pugin, one of the architects of the Houses of Parliament in London – a connection obvious from the superb neo-Gothic detailing and the sheer presence of the building, whose spire is the highest in Edinburgh.

Gladstone's Land

MAP P.30, POCKET MAP B15
477b Lawnmarket ☎ 0131 458 0200, ⓦ nts.org.uk. Daily April–Dec 10am–5pm. £7; NTS.
Tall, narrow **Gladstone's Land** is the Royal Mile's best surviving example of a typical seventeenth-century tenement. The building would have been home to various families living in cramped conditions: the well-to-do Gledstanes, who built it in 1620, are thought to have occupied the third floor. The National Trust for Scotland has carefully restored the rooms, filling them with period furnishings and fittings. The arcaded and wooden-fronted ground floor is home to a reconstructed cloth shop; pass through this and you encounter a warren of tight little staircases, tiny rooms, creaking floorboards and peek-hole windows. The finest room, on the first floor immediately above the arcade, has a marvellous renaissance painted ceiling that was only discovered in the 1930s after the building was saved from demolition.

The Writers' Museum

MAP P.30, POCKET MAP B15
Lady Stairs Close, Lawnmarket ☎ 0131 529 4901, ⓦ edinburghmuseums.org.uk. Wed–Sat 10am–5pm, Sun noon–5pm. Free.
Situated within the seventeenth-century Lady Stair's House, the

The Writers' Museum

The Writers' Museum is dedicated to Scotland's three greatest literary lions: Sir Walter Scott, Robert Louis Stevenson and Robert Burns. It's a small affair with displays of first edition copies, original manuscripts and personal effects including Burn's original writing desk, a pair of riding boots given to Stevenson by a Samoan chief, engraved with the word "Tusitala" meaning "teller of tails" and the original press used to print Scott's Waverley novels. The house's tight, winding stairs and poky, wood-panelled rooms offer an authentic and attractive flavour of the medieval Old Town.

Parliament Square

MAP P.30, POCKET MAP C15
High St

Named after Parliament House – the seventeenth-century building here that was Scotland's political chamber prior to the 1707 Act of Union – Parliament Square is an impressive and unexpected opening beside the Royal Mile that contains the High Kirk of St Giles and the Mercat Cross – a small stone structure common in Scottish burghs that would be used to make Royal pronouncements and around which markets could be held. Beside the kirk, the pattern set in the cobblestones near the main entrance to St Giles is known as the **Heart of Midlothian**, a nickname for the Edinburgh Tolbooth, which stood on this spot and was regarded as the heart of the city. The prison attached to the Tolbooth was immortalized in Sir Walter Scott's novel *Heart of Midlothian*, and you may still see locals spitting on the cobblestone heart, a continuation of the tradition of spitting on the door of the prison to ward off the evil contained therein.

High Kirk of St Giles

MAP P.30, POCKET MAP C15
High St ☏ 0131 226 0674, ⊛ stgiles cathedral.org.uk. May–Sept Mon–Fri 9am–7pm, Sat 9am–5pm, Sun 1–5pm; Oct–April Mon–Sat 9am–5pm, Sun 1–5pm. Free.

Deacon Brodie

As the real-life, late eighteenth-century inspiration for Robert Louis Stevenson's novel, *The Strange Case of Dr Jekyll and Mr Hyde*, Deacon Brodie saw no contradiction in flirting with the gutter while getting on with the day job. A highly respected councillor, master cabinet maker, locksmith and heir to his father's fortune during working hours and a drinking, gambling and womanizing debauchee come sundown, Brodie was a habitual presence in the seedy taverns of Edinburgh's darker closes.

Eventually, his bad habits caught up with him as the burden of his two mistresses, five illegitimate children and gambling debts spiralled out of control. As trusted locksmith for Edinburgh's gentry the temptation to copy keys proved too much for him and he and his criminal cohorts began targeting their properties. The raids became ever more audacious until eventually an attempt to rob the excise house was disturbed and one of the gang lost his nerve and turned himself in. Knowing that the game was up, Brodie fled to Holland but was captured and returned home to face justice. Sentenced to hang on Lawnmarket, ironically on the very gallows that he himself had designed, Brodie had one last dodge up his sleeve. Wearing a steel collar he intended to survive the noose and escape. Records show he was unsuccessful, although subsequent sightings of him in Paris enhanced his legend.

The Thistle Chapel at St. Giles church

The **High Kirk of St Giles** is the original parish church of medieval Edinburgh, from where John Knox (see page 37) launched and directed the Scottish Reformation. St Giles is often referred to as a cathedral, although it has only been the seat of a bishop on two brief and unhappy occasions in the seventeenth century. The resplendent **crown spire** of the kirk is formed from eight flying buttresses and dates back to 1485, while **inside**, the four massive piers supporting the tower were part of a Norman church built here around 1120. In the nineteenth century, St Giles was adorned with a whole series of funerary monuments on the model of London's Westminster Abbey; around the same time it acquired several attractive Pre-Raphaelite stained-glass windows designed by Edward Burne-Jones and William Morris.

Thistle Chapel

At the southeastern corner of St Giles, the **Thistle Chapel** was built by Sir Robert Lorimer in 1911 as the private chapel of the sixteen knights of the Most Noble Order of the Thistle, the highest chivalric order in Scotland. Based on St George's Chapel in Windsor, it's an exquisite piece of craftsmanship, with an elaborate ribbed vault, huge drooping bosses and extravagantly ornate stalls showing off Lorimer's bold Arts and Crafts styling.

The Real Mary King's Close

MAP P.30, POCKET MAP C15
2 Warriston's Close, High St ☏ 0131 225 0672, ⓦ realmarykingsclose.com. April–Oct daily 10am–9pm; Nov–March Mon–Thurs & Sun 10am–5pm, Fri & Sat 10am–9pm. Tours (every 15min; 1hr) £14.75.

When work on the Royal Exchange, known as the City Chambers, began in 1753, the existing tenements that overlooked **Mary King's Close** were only partially demolished to make way for the new building being constructed on top of them. The process left large sections of the houses, together with the old closes that ran alongside them, intact but entirely enclosed within the basement and cellars of the City Chambers. You can visit this rather spooky subterranean "lost city" on

tours led by costumed actors, who take you round the cold stone shells of the houses where various scenes from the Close's history have been re-created. As you'd expect, blood, plague, pestilence and ghostly apparitions are to the fore, though there is an acknowledgement of the more prosaic side of medieval life in the archaeological evidence of an urban cow byre. The tour ends with a stroll up the remarkably well-preserved close itself.

St Cecilia's Hall: Concert Room and Music Museum

MAP P.30, POCKET MAP D15
Niddry St ☎ 0131 650 2600, ⓦ ed.ac.uk/
visit/museums-galleries/st-cecilias. Tues–
Fri 10am–5pm, Sat noon–5pm. Free.
An unexpected delight located down grimy Niddry Street, Edinburgh University's luxuriously renovated **Music Museum** contains an impressive acquirement of historical musical instruments from around the world, many of which are mesmerizingly beautiful like the nineteenth-century stringed Indian *mayuri* carved into a peacock. Upstairs regular public recitals in Scotland's oldest purpose built concert hall – from 1762 – are a unique and intimate affair. See the website for what's on.

Museum of Childhood

Museum of Childhood

MAP P.30, POCKET MAP D15
42 High St ☎ 0131 529 4142, ⓦ edinburgh
museums.org.uk. Mon & Thurs–Sat
10am–5pm, Sun noon–5pm. Free.
Harking back to simpler times, the **Museum of Childhood** hosts a joyful collection of toys, clothes, dolls and bikes that kids used to cherish before the advent of plastic. Over the five small exhibition spaces there's a surprisingly large amount to see here, including a beautiful model railway scene, a room dedicated to childhood hobbies and some fancy old Victorian dollhouses.

Scottish Storytelling Centre

MAP P.30, POCKET MAP D14
43–45 High St ☎ 0131 556 9579,
ⓦ tracscotland.org/scottish-storytelling-
centre. Mon–Sat 10am–6pm, also Sun
noon–6pm in July & Aug. John Knox House
£5; Storytelling Centre free.
There are two distinct parts to the **Scottish Storytelling Centre**. One half is a stylish contemporary development containing an excellent café, the Netherbow Theatre – which hosts regular performances, often aimed at a younger audience – and an airy **Storytelling Court** with a small permanent exhibition about Scottish stories from ancient folk tales to *Harry Potter*. By contrast, **John Knox House** next door – but part of the same complex – is a fifteenth-century stone-and-timber building which, with its distinctive external staircase, overhanging upper storeys and busy pantile roof, is a classic example of the Royal Mile in its medieval heyday. Inside, the house is all low doorways, uneven floors and ornate wooden panelling; it contains a series of displays about Knox, the minister who led the Reformation in Scotland and established Calvinist Presbyterianism as the dominant religious force in the country.

John Knox

Protestant reformer **John Knox** has been credited with, or blamed for, the distinctive national characteristic of rather gloomy reserve that emerged from the Calvinist Reformation and which has cast its shadow right up to the present. Little is known about Knox's early years: he was born between 1505 and 1514 in East Lothian, and trained for the priesthood at St Andrews University. Ordained in 1540, Knox then served as a private tutor, in league with Scotland's first significant Protestant leader, **George Wishart**. After Wishart was burnt at the stake for heresy in 1546, Knox became involved with the group who had carried out the revenge murder of the Scottish primate, Cardinal David Beaton.

When Mary Tudor, a Catholic, acceded to the English throne in 1553, Knox fled to the Continent to avoid becoming embroiled in the religious turmoil. Returning two years later, he took over as spiritual leader of the Reformation, becoming minister of St Giles in Edinburgh, where he gained a reputation as a charismatic preacher. The establishment of Protestantism as the official religion of Scotland in 1560 was dependent on the forging of an alliance with **Elizabeth I**, which Knox himself rigorously championed: the swift deployment of English troops against the French garrison in Edinburgh dealt a fatal blow to Franco–Spanish hopes of re-establishing Catholicism in both Scotland and England. Although the return of **Mary, Queen of Scots** the following year placed a Catholic monarch on the Scottish throne, Knox was reputedly always able to retain the upper hand in his famous disputes with her.

Before his death in 1572, Knox began sweeping away all vestiges of episcopal control of the **Scots Kirk** and giving lay people a role of unprecedented importance. He proposed a nationwide education system, compulsory for the very young and free for the poor. His final legacy was the posthumously published *History of the Reformation of Religion in the Realm of Scotland*, a justification of his life's work.

The People's Story Museum

MAP P.30, POCKET MAP E14
Canongate Tolbooth, 163 Canongate
☏ 0131 529 4057, ⓦ edinburghmuseums.org.uk. Sept–July Wed–Sat 10am–5pm, Aug Sun noon–5pm. Free.

Dominated by a turreted steeple and an odd external box clock, the late sixteenth-century **Canongate Tolbooth** has served both as the headquarters of the burgh administration and as a prison. It now houses **The People's Story Museum**, which contains a series of display cases, dense information boards and rather old-fashioned tableaux dedicated to the everyday life and work of Edinburgh's population through the centuries. This isn't one of Edinburgh's essential museums, but it does have a down-to-earth reality often missing from places dedicated to high culture or famous historical characters.

Museum of Edinburgh

MAP P.30, POCKET MAP F14
142–146 Canongate ☏ 0131 529 4143,
ⓦ edinburghmuseums.org.uk. Mon & Thurs–Sat 10am–5pm, also Sun noon–5pm. Free.

Housing the city's principal collection devoted to local history, the **Museum of Edinburgh** is as interesting for the labyrinthine

Literary Edinburgh

While Edinburgh's fine skyline, world renowned festivals, art galleries and architectural heritage draw in an exponentially increasing number of visitors every year, it is arguably literary tourism that is having the city's most impressive renaissance. A new breed of writers who, like the classic novelists of the past, have found inspiration among Edinburgh's ancient howfs (pub in Old Scots), tight closes and grand Georgian buildings are enticing visitors to seek out specific tour companies that will escort them to their favourite book locations.

The **Harry Potter** tours are enduringly popular. Take a stroll down Victoria Street, the inspiration for **Diagon Alley** where there's now a dedicated Potter shop, **Diagon House** (see page 52) and then enter the Greyfriars Kirkyard to look for the final resting place of Thomas Riddell, AKA Lord Voldemort. Behind the wall is **George Heriot's School** (see page 47) that gave rise to the concept of Hogwarts School of Witchcraft and Wizardry. Another tombstone here displays the name William McGonagall, a probable name source for the Hogwarts Professor, played in the film adaption by Maggie Smith who coincidently acted out a scene in this very kirkyard as the star of Muriel Spark's **The Prime of Miss Jean Brodie**.

Cult fiction novels have their fair share of pilgrims too. Irvine Welsh's **Trainspotting** film adaptions show off some of Edinburgh's more iconic cityscapes while also introducing some of its less savoury localities like Leith's notorious **Banana flats** (see page 99), used as Sick Boy's drug den.

The majority of Edinburgh's literary acclaim is reserved for Scotland's Romanticist authors however. None more so than that of Sir Walter Scott, whose accolades include the main station (Waverley) and a football team (Heart of Midlothian), both named after his novels, while the Scott Monument (see page 70) is

the largest dedication to an author in the world. Naturally he also features prominently in the Writer's Museum (see page 33) collection alongside Robert Louis Stevenson and national poet, Robert Burns who also have bronze statues around the city. Look out for Stevenson's *Kidnapped* bronze featuring the story's two main protagonists on the edge of Corstorphine hill, sight of their final parting; conveniently for sightseers, also on the airport bus route.

Edinburgh's passion for literature is not just inward looking. The relatively recent additions to the Royal Mile

of the Scottish Storytelling Centre (see page 36) and the Scottish Poetry library (see page 40) have widened the focus internationally and, together with the thriving Edinburgh International Book Festival (see page 145) in August helped earn Edinburgh the first UNESCO City of Literature designation.

Tours

EDINBURGH LITERARY PUB TOUR
Departs from outside the Beehive Inn, 18–20 Grassmarket ☎ 0800 169 7410, Ⓦ edinburghliterarypubtour.co.uk. 7.30pm; lasts 2–3hrs: Jan–March Fri & Sun, April & Oct Thurs–Sun, May–Sept daily, Nov & Dec Fri. £15, or £13 online.

A pub crawl where you'll be introduced to the scenes, characters and words of the major figures of Scottish literature. Hosted by a pair of well-seasoned actors, you'll have the opportunity to procure a swift ale at each of the four pubs visited as you walk/crawl from the Grassmarket to Rose Street.

POTTER TRAIL
Departs from Greyfriars Bobby statue, Candlemaker Row Ⓦ pottertrail.com. Nov–Feb Wed–Sun 3pm, otherwise daily at 3pm (lasts 1hr 15min). Free but donations welcomed. No booking required.

A muggle-friendly tour of all the Harry Potter sights. With wand in hand – given out at the start – you'll encounter the gravestones, cobbled lanes and ancient buildings that inspired the books while being thoroughly entertained by your enthusiastic wizard guide.

REBUS TOURS
Departs from outside Royal Oak Pub, 1 Infirmary St ☎ 0131 553 7473, Ⓦ rebustours.com. Every Sat noon (lasts 2hrs). £10.

Informative tours that take in the inspirations and locations of Ian Rankin's Detective Rebus novels with plenty of history added to the mix.

Canongate Kirk

2011, when Prince William's cousin Zara Phillips married England rugby player Mike Tindall. The kirk has a modesty rarely seen in churches built in later centuries, with a graceful curved facade and a bow-shaped gable to the rear. The surrounding churchyard provides an attractive and tranquil stretch of green in the heart of the Old Town and affords fine views of Calton Hill; it also happens to be one of the city's most exclusive cemeteries – well-known internees include the political economist Adam Smith, Mrs Agnes McLehose (better known as Robert Burns's "Clarinda") and Robert Fergusson, regarded by some as Edinburgh's greatest poet, despite his death at the age of 24. Fergusson's headstone was donated by Burns, a fervent admirer, and a statue of the young poet can be seen just outside the kirk gates.

network of wood-panelled rooms within as it is for its rather quirky array of artefacts. These do, however, include a number of items of real historical significance, in particular the **National Convention**, the petition for religious freedom drawn up on a deerskin parchment in 1638, and the original plans for the layout of the New Town drawn by James Craig chosen by the city council after a competition in 1767.

Canongate Kirk

MAP P.30, POCKET MAP F14
153 Canongate ☎ 0131 556 3515, ⓦ canongatekirk.org.uk. May–Sept Mon–Sat 10.30am–4.30pm, Sun 12.30–4.30pm, depending on volunteer staff and church services. Free.

Built to house the congregation expelled from Holyrood Abbey when the latter was commandeered by James VII (James II in England), **Canongate Kirk** is the church used by the Queen when she's at Holyrood and was the location for Britain's "other royal wedding" of

Scottish Poetry Library

MAP P.30, POCKET MAP F14
5 Crichton's Close, Canongate ☎ 0131 557 2876, ⓦ scottishpoetrylibrary.org.uk. Tues–Fri 10am–5pm, Sat 10am–4pm. Free.

A small island of modern architectural eloquence amid a cacophony of large-scale developments, the **Scottish Poetry Library**'s attractive design harmoniously combines brick, oak, glass, Caithness stone and blue ceramic tiles while incorporating a section of an old city wall. Inside you'll encounter Scotland's most comprehensive collection of native poetry, and visitors are free to read the books, periodicals and leaflets found on the shelves, or listen to recordings of poetry in the nation's three tongues, Lowland Scots, Scots Gaelic and English. The library's main focus is on modern and post War Scottish poetry; however, with over 45,000 items on the shelves there's plenty choice of historical and international verse, particularly European, many examples of which have been translated into English.

Shops

Cavanagh Antiques

MAP P.30, POCKET MAP C14

49 Cockburn St ☎ 0131 226 3391. Mon–Sat 11am–5pm.

Long established, poky shop crammed with a consistently good range of interesting items. Particularly good for jewellery.

Coda Music

MAP P.30, POCKET MAP C15

12 Bank Street ☎ 0131 622 7246, ⓦ codamusic.co.uk. Mon–Sat 9.30am–5.30pm, Sun 11am–5pm.

Well stocked outlet specializing in folk music CDs and vinyl – in the broadest sense of the term – with a modern, eclectic range of Scottish and emerging artists, some classic world music titles and a few bagpiping CDs to keep the place ticking over.

Robert Graham

MAP P.30, POCKET MAP E15

254 Canongate ☎ 0131 556 2791, ⓦ robertgraham1874.com. Mon–Wed 10.30am–6pm, Thurs & Fri 10.30am–7pm, Sat 10.30am–6.30pm, Sun noon–5.30pm.

There's no end of opportunity to buy whisky in Edinburgh but this little business, dating back to the Victorian era is a must. Look out for the Treasurer 1874 Reserve Cask; using the Solera system of fractional blending, the cask is never allowed to empty and the blend is therefore of the widest range of ages.

Royal Mile Market

MAP P.30, POCKET MAP D15

Tron Kirk, 122 High St ☎ 0131 260 9971, ⓦ royalmilemarket.co.uk. Sun–Fri 10am–6pm, Sat 10am–7pm.

A popular diversion where local artisans and cheap accessories traders thrive on the Royal Mile's bountiful foot-traffic in this small market, housed inside the old Tron Kirk.

Underground Solu'shn

MAP P.30, POCKET MAP C15

9 Cockburn St ☎ 0131 226 2242, ⓦ undergroundsolushn.com. Mon–Wed & Fri–Sat 10am–6pm, Thurs 10am–7pm, Sun noon–6pm.

Edinburgh's last remaining record shop dedicated to dance and electronic music with a huge selection of vinyl and CDs, plus some nice clothing and accessories. There's a row of decks so you can try before you buy.

Cafés

Baba Budan

MAP P.30, POCKET MAP E14

Arch 12, 17 East Market St ☎ 07753 742550, ⓦ bababudan.co.uk. Mon & Tues 7.30am–4pm, Wed–Fri 7.30am–5pm, Sat–Sun 9.30am–5pm

Billing itself as a "Donutterie", this much talked about new addition to Edinburgh's unstoppable café culture offers crispy fresh doughnuts with imaginative fillings to dunk in your artisan latte.

Colonnades

MAP P.30, POCKET MAP C15

The Signet Library, Parliament Square ☎ 0131 226 1064, ⓦ thesignetlibrary. co.uk. Mon–Fri 1–5pm, Sun 11am–5pm.

Royal Mile Market

Afternoon tea in the plushest of surroundings and a giant gourmet leap above the standard egg and cress sandwiches. Here it's pea and truffle panna cotta, rhubarb bavarois and, naturally, scones. Careful not to splutter your Earl Grey when the bill arrives: £30 per person.

Deacon's House Café

MAP P.30, POCKET MAP C15
Brodie's Close, 304 Lawnmarket ☎ 0131 226 1894. Sept–Feb daily 9am–5pm.
Look out for the life-sized mannequin of Deacon Brodie (see page 34) at the entrance to this café's close. Both the period decor and outside seating area, not to mention the light, crumbly scones, make it a welcome respite from the frenetic Royal Mile.

The Edinburgh Larder

MAP P.30, POCKET MAP D15
15 Blackfriars St ☎ 0131 556 6922, ⓦ edinburghlarder.co.uk; Sept–Feb Mon–Fri 8am–5pm, Sat & Sun 9am–5pm, March–July daily 8am–5pm; Aug daily 7am–10pm.

Overwhelmingly popular café-diner dishing up top notch breakfast favourites like the Full Scottish for £9.50 and the scrambled egg, salmon and bacon on toast for £7. There's also gluten free cakes, soups, sandwiches and daily specials that focus on local, seasonal produce.

Mimi's Little Bakehouse

MAP P.30, POCKET MAP E15
250 Canongate ☎ 0131 556 6632, ⓦ mimisbakehouse.com. Mon–Fri 8am–6pm, Sat–Sun 10am–6pm.
Small, friendly café specializing in cakes and scones – some of the lightest you'll ever taste. Generous breakfasts and lunches served too.

Tempo Tea Bar

MAP P.30, POCKET MAP D14
7 East Market St ☎ 0131 556 4763, ⓦ tempoteabar.com. Daily 11am–7pm.
Friendly café specializing in bubble tea, a Taiwanese originated drink – made from green tea, milk, natural flavours and tapioca balls – that professes all manner of health benefits.

Monteiths restaurant and cocktail bar

Restaurants

Amber

MAP P.30, POCKET MAP B15
354 Castlehill ☎ 0131 477 8477, ⓦ amber-restaurant.co.uk. Mon–Thurs & Sun 10am–8.30pm, Fri & Sat noon–9pm.
Connected to The Scotch Whisky Experience (see page 32), here you can explore the nation's larder with the Taste of Scotland menu featuring a trio of starters and mains including haggis bonbons for £33.50. There's also a whisky sommelier on hand to suggest accompanying drams for each course.

David Bann

MAP P.30, POCKET MAP E15
56–58 St Mary's St ☎ 0131 556 5888, ⓦ davidbann.com. Mon–Thurs noon–10pm, Fri noon–10.30pm, Sat 11am–10.30pm, Sun 11am–10pm.
Fine dining, vegetarian style, with a tried and tested menu. There are a few unconventional dishes offered here, such as the quinoa chilli and tortilla chips with chocolate sauce (£13) and the beetroot, apple and blue cheese pudding (£14) – both main courses.

La Garrigue

MAP P.30, POCKET MAP D14
31 Jeffrey St ☎ 0131 557 3032, ⓦ lagarrigue.co.uk. Daily noon–2.30pm & 6–9.30pm.
A double AA Rosette-awarded restaurant, with a menu and wine list dedicated to the produce and traditions of the Languedoc region of France. For unmistakably authentic paysan cuisine, aim for the cassoulet, part of the £14.50 two-course lunch menu.

Monteiths

MAP P.30, POCKET MAP D15
61 High St ☎ 0131 557 0330, ⓦ monteithsrestaurant.co.uk. Daily noon–1am, food served daily noon–10.30pm.
Entered through an enticing vennel adorned with fairy lights and twisted willow canes,

Vegetarian dining at David Bann

Monteith's is a sophisticated part restaurant, part cocktail bar. Not great for vegetarians, the focus is heavily on melt in the mouth permutations of venison and beef. Mains start at £18.

Ondine

MAP P.30, POCKET MAP C15
2 George IV Bridge ☎ 0131 226 1888, ⓦ ondinerestaurant.co.uk. Mon–Sat noon–3pm & 5.30–10pm.
Dedicated seafood restaurant from Edinburgh-born Roy Brett, once Rick Stein's main chef in Padstow, turning out sublime dishes using native shellfish and fish from sustainable sources. Two-course lunch and pre-theatre menus cost £19.

Wedgwood the Restaurant

MAP P.30, POCKET MAP E14
267 Canongate ☎ 0131 558 8737, ⓦ wedgwoodtherestaurant.co.uk. Mon–Sat noon–3pm & 6–10pm.
This small, award-winning fine-dining restaurant with in-house forager creatively plates all the best of Scotland's land, rivers and seas. There's so much choice on the à la carte menu that they offer "deciding time" – canapés and

The Witchery by the Castle

champagne – while you peruse the menu. The mains here begin at £16, although the £15 lunch deal is the best value, all with seasonal freshness guaranteed.

The Witchery by the Castle

MAP P.30, POCKET MAP B15
352 Castlehill ☎ 0131 225 5613, Ⓦ thewitchery.com. Daily noon–11.30pm.
An upmarket restaurant that only Edinburgh could create, set in magnificently over-the-top medieval surroundings full of Gothic wood panelling and heavy stonework, all a mere broomstick-hop from the Castle. The à la carte menu is as ostentatious as the surroundings, with wallet-draining lobster and lamb wellington on offer; however, there are good-value set menus from £22 for two courses.

Pubs and bars

The Banshee Labyrinth

MAP P.30, POCKET MAP D15
29–35 Niddry St ☎ 0131 558 8209, Ⓦ the bansheelabyrinth.com. Daily 10am–3am.

"Scotland's most haunted pub", apparently. While glasses have been known to shatter of their own accord, this impeccably dark and dingy bolthole is mostly haunted by metal heads and tourists. Built as it is into a chunk of prime South Bridge vaults, there are plenty of unsavoury nooks and crannies to enjoy the live metal, punk, occasional electronica, karaoke and B-movie cinema.

The City Café

MAP P.30, POCKET MAP D15
19 Blair St ☎ 0131 220 0125, Ⓦ citycafe edinburgh.co.uk. Daily 9am–1am.
The American-diner-minimalist grand dame of Edinburgh style bars, and a home from home for fashionistas, wannabes and DJs in the late 80s and 90s. The competition may be much stiffer these days, but it's still a pre-club fixture.

Deacon Brodie's Tavern

MAP P.30, POCKET MAP C15
435 Lawnmarket ☎ 0131 225 6531, Ⓦ nicholsonspubs.co.uk. Mon–Sat 11am–1am, Sun 10am–midnight.

Lively, two-floored historic Victorian pub with a gorgeous ornate ceiling. Throngs with tourists and locals particularly at lunchtime.

The Devil's Advocate

MAP P.30, POCKET MAP C15
9 Advocates Close ⓣ 0131 225 4465. Daily noon–1am. ⓦ devilsadvocate edinburgh.co.uk.
Atmospheric bar in a converted Victorian pump house hidden halfway down a close and specializing in exotic whisky. Tends to fill at the end of the working day with young office workers sipping cocktails.

Halfway House

MAP P.30, POCKET MAP D14
24 Fleshmarket Close ⓣ 0131 225 7101. Mon–Sat 11am–11pm, Sun 12.30am–11pm.
Formerly a second home for Scotsman hacks when the newspaper was based at South Bridge, this tiny pub halfway up the steep, narrow close between the train station and the Royal Mile, is a handy place to stop and catch your breath. Lots of real ales and a few simple bar meals on offer, like cullen skink for £5.

Jolly Judge

MAP P.30, POCKET MAP B15
7 James Court ⓣ 0131 225 2669, ⓦ jollyjudge.co.uk. Mon & Fri–Sat noon–midnight, Tues–Thurs noon–11pm, Sun 12.30–11pm.
Traditional pub in a basement at the end of a windy vennel that always has the big-name Scottish ales on tap and, come winter, an open fire in fine fettle.

The Malt Shovel

MAP P.30, POCKET MAP C15
11–15 Cockburn St ⓣ 0131 225 6843, ⓦ maltshovelinn-edinburgh.co.uk. Sun–Thurs 11am–midnight, Fri–Sat 11am–1am
Spacious Georgian-era pub on the edge of the Old Town specializing in whisky – there are over 150 on offer. There's also a decent real ale rotation and no nonsense pub grub available.

Vino

MAP P.30, POCKET MAP E14
27 East Market St ⓣ 0131 629 4282, ⓦ vinowines.co.uk. Wed 4–8pm, Thurs–Fri 4–10pm, Sat 1–10pm, Sun 1–8pm.
Independent wine bar and shop in the attractively renovated arches under Jeffrey Street. A great stop before heading out to a bring-your-own bottle restaurant.

The World's End

MAP P.30, POCKET MAP E14
2–8 High St ⓣ 0131 556 3628, ⓦ worldsend-edinburgh.co.uk. Mon–Fri 11am–1am. Sat–Sat–Sun 10am–1am
A rowdy old howf that gets its name from the Tolbooth that used to sit outside, which to the poorest folk of Edinburgh was too expensive to pass through, hence to them it was the world's end.

Clubs and venues

Monkey Barrel Comedy

MAP P.30, POCKET MAP D15
9 Blair St ⓣ 0845 500 1056, ⓦ monkeybarrelcomedy.com. Daily shows start 8.30pm.
Small, one-room venue showcasing predominately new and emerging acts. With entry from £3 to £12 and a reasonably priced bar, you're in for a cheap night out.

Whistlebinkies

MAP P.30, POCKET MAP D15
4–6 South Bridge ⓣ 0131 557 5114, ⓦ whistlebinkies.com. Daily 11.30am–3am. Entry free except after midnight on Fri & Sat when it's £4.
An Edinburgh stalwart and one of the most reliable places to find live music every night of the week (and often afternoons too), or just to hunker down in some of the lesser haunted South Bridge vaults. On the whole it's local indie bands or rock and pop covers, though there are some folk evenings as well.

South of the Royal Mile

The southern section of the Old Town has two distinct levels. The upper belongs to a pair of Georgian bridges (George IV and South Bridge) that feed off from the Royal Mile, Chambers Street – home to the venerable National Museum of Scotland – and George Heriot's School, a glorious early seventeenth-century pile tucked inside the remnants of the old Flodden wall. To reach the lower section most visitors find themselves enticed off the George IV Bridge by the curving incline of photogenic Victoria Street, with its colourful arched boutique shop fronts. At the foot of hill the street opens onto the Grassmarket, a large square filled with congenial pavement cafés, pubs and restaurants. In the early evenings, local barflies rub shoulders with hen and stag parties, who eventually stagger eastwards to the late bars and clubs along the Cowgate to the east.

Victoria Street

Curving downhill from George IV Bridge towards the Grassmarket via West Bow, photogenic **Victoria Street** is an unusual two-tier thoroughfare, with colourful arcaded shops below and a pedestrian terrace high above. The street

Colourful shops on Victoria Street

has retained an aesthetic grip on itself, hosting a string of appealing offbeat, independent boutiques, a cheesemonger and an old bookseller.

Built between 1829 and 1834, Victoria Street was part of a series of improvements to the Old Town; access to Lawnmarket from the Grassmarket had previously been up a steep and often slippery incline at West Bow. All this changed with the mass demolition of rows of tenements all the way up today's Victoria Street to cut a path onto the newly built George IV Bridge.

The Grassmarket

Used as the city's cattle market from 1477 to 1911, the **Grassmarket** is an open, partly cobbled area, which despite being girdled by tall tenements offers an unexpected view north up to the precipitous walls of the Castle. Come springtime, it's often sunny enough for cafés to put tables and chairs along the pavement; however, such Continental aspirations are a bit of a diversion as the Grassmarket is best remembered as the location of Edinburgh's public gallows – the spot is marked by a tiny garden. The notorious serial killers William Burke and William Hare had their lair in a now-vanished close just off the western end of the Grassmarket, and for a long time before its relatively recent gentrification there was a seamy edge to the place, with brothels, drinking dens and shelters for down-and-outs.

The Grassmarket's two-sided character is still on view, with a lively drinking scene of an evening, while by day you can admire the architectural quirks and a series of interesting shops and restaurants plus, on Saturdays, the food and craft market.

The Cowgate

Leading eastwards from the Grassmarket is the **Cowgate**, one of Edinburgh's oldest surviving streets. It was also once one of the city's most prestigious addresses, but the construction of the great **viaducts** of George IV Bridge and South Bridge entombed it below street level, condemning it to decay and neglect and leading the

nineteenth-century poet, Alexander Smith, to declare: "the condition of the inhabitants is as little known to respectable Edinburgh as are the habits of moles, earthworms, and the mining population." Various nightclubs and Festival venues have established themselves here – on Friday and Saturday nights the street heaves with revellers – but it remains a slightly insalubrious spot.

George Heriot's School

MAP P.48, POCKET MAP B16
Lauriston Place ☏ 0131 229 7263, ⓦ george-heriots.com. Occasionally open to the public, check website for details. Free.
Built with funds from the benevolent legacy of goldsmith, turned philanthropist **George Heriot** in the mid-seventeenth century to provide charitable schooling for the "puir, faitherless bairns" of the city. The resulting Renaissance building standing just west of the Greyfriars Kirk was the first large-scale construction outside of the city walls. Four main towers, each with four turrets, corner an inner quadrangle entered via the

The Connolly Connection

Among Edinburgh's multitude of famous and infamous sons, one of the most obscure – and perhaps most unlikely – remains **James Connolly**, commander-in-chief of the **Easter 1916 rising** which eventually led to the formation of the Irish Republic. With no monument save for a small plaque at the foot of George IV Bridge in the Cowgate, few among Edinburgh's tourist hordes are likely aware that Connolly was born and raised there in the bowels of Edinburgh's Old Town. A pivotal figure in emerging socialist and trade union movements in Scotland, Ireland and beyond, including Keir Hardie's Independent Labour Party (a forerunner of the contemporary **Labour Party**), Connolly came to believe that armed insurrection was the only way to free Ireland from the British Empire, and his prominent role in the rising ultimately led to execution by firing squad (infamously while badly wounded and tied to a chair). While the uprising resulted in heavy casualties on both sides, as well as many civilian deaths, and the independent state that eventually emerged wasn't the socialist utopia he had dreamed of, his vision of freedom and equality for all has remained an inspiration to many, not least **John Lennon**, who quoted Connolly's writings on female emancipation as a cue for "Woman is the Nigger of the World".

bell-topped clock tower on the north end. Its part castle part palatial look became the inspiration for numerous other independent schools around the city and more recently, Hogwarts from the *Harry Potter* series. Today, it's one of Edinburgh's more exclusive private schools and visiting is usually only possible during September's Open Doors day (see doorsopendays.org.uk).

Anatomical Museum

MAP P.48, POCKET MAP E6
Doorway 3, Medical School, Teviot Place
T 0131 650 1000, W ed.ac.uk. Aug–May last Sat of the month 10am–4pm.

Edinburgh University's morbidly fascinating three-hundred-year-old collection is displayed at the **Anatomical Museum**. Expect phrenology masks, body sections and skeletal remains including those of infamous serial killer, William Burke, whose skin forms the cover of a notebook residing at the nearby Surgeons' Hall Museums (see page 51). Entered by passing between the two elephant skeletons standing in the splendid vaulted foyer, the museum is housed in a large sky-lit rectangular room with numerous glass cabinets. There's a decent natural history contingent with a few primate skeletons and a huge narwhal's tooth, but the core of the collection relates to human anatomy. The more gory items like their jarred foetal abnormalities are locked away in the Skull Room (by prior arrangement if you can prove you are doing legitimate research).

Greyfriars Kirk

MAP P.48, POCKET MAP C16
1 Greyfriars T 0131 225 1900,
W greyfriarskirk.com. April–Oct Mon–Fri 10.30am–4.30pm, Sat 11am–2pm; winter visits can be arranged by phone. Free.

Greyfriars Kirk was built in 1620 on land that had belonged to a Franciscan convent, though little of

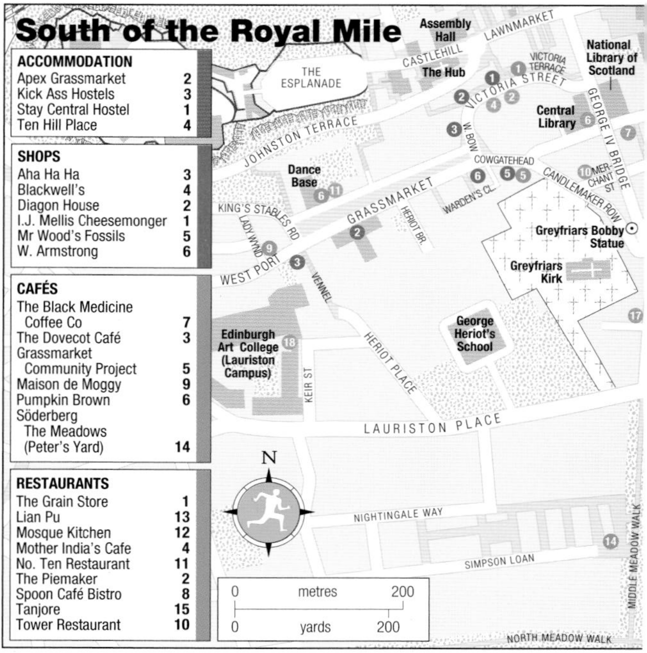

Greyfriars Bobby

The small statue of **Greyfriars Bobby** at the junction of George IV Bridge and Candlemaker Row must rank as one of Edinburgh's more mawkish tourist attractions. The legend goes that Bobby was a **Skye terrier** acquired as a working dog by a police constable named John Gray. When Gray died in 1858, Bobby was found a few days later sitting on his grave, a vigil he maintained until his death fourteen years later. In the process, he became an Edinburgh celebrity, fed and cared for by locals who gave him a special collar to prevent him being impounded as a stray. The statue was modelled from life and erected soon after his death. Bobby's legendary dedication easily lent itself to children's books and was eventually picked up by Disney, whose 1961 feature film hammed up the story and ensured that streams of tourists have paid their respects ever since.

the original late Gothic-style building remains. A fire in the mid-nineteenth century led to significant rebuilding and the installation of the first **organ** in a Presbyterian church in Scotland; today's magnificent instrument, by Peter Collins, arrived in 1990.

Outside, the kirkyard has a fine collection of seventeenth-century gravestones and mausoleums including the grave mourned over by the world-famous canine, Greyfriars Bobby. Visited regularly by ghost tours, the kirkyard was known for **grave-robbing** as freshly interred bodies were exhumed and sold to the nearby medical school (a crime taken to a higher level by the notorious

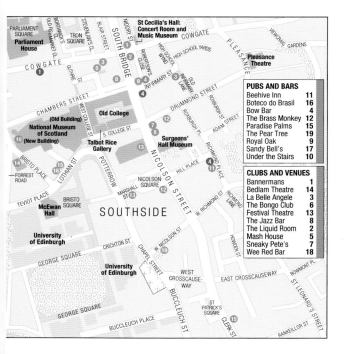

PUBS AND BARS

Beehive Inn	11
Boteco do Brasil	16
Bow Bar	4
The Brass Monkey	12
Paradise Palms	15
The Pear Tree	19
Royal Oak	9
Sandy Bell's	17
Under the Stairs	10

CLUBS AND VENUES

Bannermans	1
Bedlam Theatre	14
La Belle Angele	3
The Bongo Club	6
Festival Theatre	13
The Jazz Bar	8
The Liquid Room	2
Mash House	5
Sneaky Pete's	7
Wee Red Bar	18

National Museum of Scotland

Burke and Hare, who bypassed the graveyards by simply murdering the victims before selling them). More significantly, the kirkyard was the setting, in 1638, for the signing of the **National Covenant**, a dramatic act of defiance by the Presbyterian Scots against Charles I's attempts to impose episcopal worship on the country. In an undemocratic age, thousands of townsfolk and noblemen signed the original document at Greyfriars; copies were then made and sent around the country, with some three hundred thousand names being added.

National Museum of Scotland

MAP P.48, POCKET MAP C16
Chambers St ☎ 0300 123 6789, ⓦ nms. ac.uk. Daily 10am–5pm; guided tours 11am, 1pm & 3pm (1hr; free). Free.
The **National Museum of Scotland** is essentially two distinct museums, internally connected to each other: the unorthodox **modern sandstone building** on the corner of George IV Bridge (the Museum of Scotland) houses collections of Scottish heritage, while the much older **Venetian-style palace (the Royal Museum)** offers a more global perspective of antiquity, geology and natural history. Inside, the wealth of exhibits is enough to

occupy days of your time, but as entry is free you'll be able to dip in and out at leisure or during rain showers. Parents will also find the place a useful sanctuary since there are numerous child-friendly rooms, interactive exhibits and cafés.

The Royal Museum

Modelled on the former Crystal Palace in London, with a spectacular cast-iron interior, the **Old Building** packs in a bedazzling array of artefacts, covering natural history, world culture, geology and technology. The exhibits are housed over three levels surrounding the **Grand Gallery**, a huge central atrium whose beautiful limestone floor turns out to be teeming with fossils, predominantly ammonites. One stand-out exhibit, by the main concourse, is the gruesome **Millennium Clock Tower**, a jumble of cogs, chains and wheels modelled in the form of a Gothic cathedral, with gargoyles and sinister-looking figurines representing characters from twentieth-century politics.

The **Natural World Gallery** is particularly fine, too, inhabiting all tiers of the museum's eastern end with numerous re-created animals hanging top to bottom from the rafters and a fearsome T-rex skeleton at the entrance.

The Museum of Scotland

Given its confusing and unconventional layout, you might want to pick up a free map before tackling the new building's **Scottish galleries**, which detail the history of Scotland from its geological formation through to the present day. In between, there's a wealth of remarkably well-preserved medieval exhibits – religious, regal and day-to-day objects – on display in the **Kingdom of the Scots**, including the exquisitely idiosyncratic **Lewis chessmen**. Moving forward in time, **Scotland Transformed** offers an insight into the Union of Crowns and the crushed Jacobite rebellions, leading up to the Industrial Revolution – evoked by an unmissable life-size working model of a steam-driven Newcomen Atmospheric Engine. Designed in 1712, it foreshadows Scotland's role as covered in the next section, **Industry and Empire**, where you can see a full-size steam locomotive, the *Ellesmere*, highlighting the fact that in the nineteenth century Scotland was building more railway engines than anywhere else in the world.

Surgeons' Hall Museum

MAP P.48, POCKET MAP D16
Nicolson St, between nos. 14 & 16 ☎ 0131 527 1711, ⊕ museum.rcsed.ac.uk. Daily 10am–5pm. £6.50.

Surgeons' Hall, the former headquarters of the Royal College of Surgeons, is a handsome, iconic temple with a stately columned facade built by William Playfair (1790–1857), one of Edinburgh's greatest architects. Housed round the back is one of the city's most unusual and morbidly compelling museums. In the eighteenth and nineteenth centuries, Edinburgh was a leading centre of medical and anatomical research, nurturing world-famous pioneers such as James Young Simpson, founder of anaesthesia, and Joseph Lister, the father of modern surgery.

The **history of surgery** takes up one part of the museum, with intriguing exhibits ranging from early surgical tools to a pocketbook covered with the leathered skin of serial killer William Burke. Another room has an array of gruesome instruments illustrating the history of dentistry, while the third and most remarkable part of the museum, the elegant **Playfair Hall**, contains an array of specimens and jars from the college's anatomical and pathological collections dating back to the eighteenth century.

Old College and Talbot Rice Gallery

MAP P.48, POCKET MAP D16
South Bridge ☎ 0131 650 2210, ⊕ www.trg.ed.ac.uk. Tues–Sat noon–5pm. Free.

Designed by Edinburgh's famous New Town architects, Robert Adam and, after he died, William Playfair, the resulting Old College is an aesthetically pleasing symmetrical orgy of sandstone, pillars, arcades and domes surrounding a featureless quadrangle.

At the far end of the building is the University's Talbot Rice Gallery, set up in the seventies to foster links and collaborations between students, academics and world-renowned artists. For the visitor there are three distinct exhibition spaces of predominantly contemporary art on show although the archived collection here has amassed over twenty two thousand pieces. Gallery one concentrates on new solo exhibitions on a certain theme usually by a Scottish artist. Gallery two is the most eye catching with its glass cupola and rich Georgian interior, the displays here are historic, academic and experimental and include the university's Torrie Collection, an outstanding body of nineteenth-century work ranging from Dutch and Flemish landscapes to Renaissance bronzes. Gallery three is dedicated to supporting early career and experimental artists and exhibitions are often student curated.

Shops

Aha Ha Ha

MAP P.48, POCKET MAP B16

99 West Bow ☎ 0131 220 5252, ⓦ ahaha.
co.uk. Mon–Sat 10am–6pm. Sun
11am–5pm.

A classic, old school joke shop
turning out magic tricks, costumes,
pranks and, naturally, fake poo.
Its sister shop, Hijinks around
the corner on the Grassmarket
specializes in period costumes and
masquerade masks.

Blackwell's

MAP P.48, POCKET MAP D16

53–62 South Bridge ☎ 0131 622 8222,
ⓦ blackwell.co.uk. Mon, Tues, Thurs &
Fri 9am–8pm, Wed 9.30am–8pm, Sat
9am–6pm, Sun noon–6pm.

Rambling, multi-floored bookseller
with a strong – although far from
exclusive – focus on academic
tomes. You'll also find many
volumes and travel guides relating
to Scotland.

Diagon House

MAP P.48, POCKET MAP B15

40 Victoria St ☎ 0131 226 5882. Mon–Sat
10am–10pm, Sun 10am–8pm.

An essential stop for any Harry
Potter devotee looking for wands,
capes, stuffed owls or scarves. Look
out for the large Nagini snake
hanging from the ceiling.

I.J. Mellis Cheesemonger

MAP P.48, POCKET MAP B15

30a Victoria St, Old Town ☎ 0131 226
6215, ⓦ mellischeese.co.uk. Mon–Wed
9.30am–7pm, Thurs–Sat 9.30am–7pm, Sun
11am–6.30pm.

Founded in 1993, Mellis' Old
Town shop is charmingly kitted
out in a Victorian style and well
stocked with expertly conditioned
farmhouse and artisan cheeses from
Britain, Ireland and, to a lesser
extent, the Continent.

Mr Wood's Fossils

MAP P.48, POCKET MAP B16

5 Cowgatehead ☎ 0131 220 1344, ⓦ mr
woodsfossils.co.uk. Daily 10am–5.30pm.

An internationally acclaimed dealer
of fossils, ambers and meteorites.
The displays are fascinating and
extensive with items to suit all
budgets from cheap ammonites to
dinosaur bones.

W. Armstrong

MAP P.48, POCKET MAP B16

83 Grassmarket ☎ 0131 220 5557,
ⓦ armstrongsvintage.co.uk. Mon–Thurs
10am–5.30pm, Fri & Sat 10am–6pm, Sun
noon–6pm.

A real treasure trove of vintage
and retro fashion, this small chain
is like a museum; stuffed to the
gunwales with items encompassing
everything from pre-war civvies to
the static-inducing nylon wear of
the 1970s.

Cafés

The Black Medicine Coffee Co

MAP P.48, POCKET MAP D16

2 Nicholson St ☎ 0131 557 6269,
ⓦ blackmed.co.uk. Mon–Sat 8am–8pm,
Sun 9am–7pm.

Just adjacent to Edinburgh Uni's
Old College, this cosy coffee shop
with its attractive Victorian interior
and handcrafted wooden tables is a
hub for the resident academics.

The Dovecot Café

MAP P.48, POCKET MAP D15

10 Infirmary St ☎ 0131 550 3660,
ⓦ dovecotstudios.com. Mon–Sat
10.30am–5.30pm.

Contemporary artisan café with
attached and affiliated art gallery.
Serves healthy light lunches of
soups, salads and sandwiches plus
excellent coffee.

Grassmarket Community Project

MAP P.48, POCKET MAP C16

86 Candlemaker Row ☎ 0131 225 3626,
ⓦ grassmarket.org. Mon–Sat 9am–4pm,
Sun 10am–4pm.

Appealing not-for-profit café in the purpose built local community centre providing excellent home-made cakes and light lunches. The interior is all white and bright thanks to the double storey glass frontage and roof lights.

Maison de Moggy

MAP P.48, POCKET MAP A16
17–19 West Port ☏ 0131 629 5530,
ⓦ maisondemoggy.com. Daily 10.45am–6.30pm. Entry £7, under-10s not allowed. Reservation advised.

Edinburgh's contribution to the cat café craze, this niche redoubt allows you to pass one therapeutic hour – the length of each session – with a clowder of pedigree pussycats and a cup of locally produced coffee.

Peter's Yard

MAP P.48, POCKET MAP E6
27 Simpson Loan ☏ 0131 228 5876,
ⓦ petersyard.com. Mon–Fri 7.30am–6pm, Sat & Sun 9am–6pm.

A Swedish outfit with the bread ovens on view, baskets of loaves and buns out front and probably the best coffee in town.

Pumpkin Brown

MAP P.48. POCKET MAP D5
16 Grassmarket ☏ 0131 629 1720,
ⓦ pumpkinbrown.com. Daily 10am–6pm.

An assiduous bastion to the vegan cause, this petite café's artistically prismatic breakfasts and salads will send any self-respecting Instagrammer reaching for their smart phone. Every dish is a superfood feeding frenzy like the Green Goddess Chia Pot made up of green tea powder, chia seeds and raspberry coulis. There's a strong emphasis on the benefits of raw ingredients within the salad menu but you can also tuck into some hearty, wholesome hot dishes in this café like the mushroom bourguignon or spicy tomato beanballs for just inside of a tenner.

Restaurants

The Grain Store

MAP P.48, POCKET MAP B15
30 Victoria St ☏ 0131 225 7635,
ⓦ grainstore-restaurant.co.uk. Mon–Sat noon–2.30pm & 6–9.45pm, Sun 6–9.30pm.

Decades-long Victoria Street fixture and a haven amid the bustle of the Old Town, with intimate stone walls and soft lighting. Combines top-quality modern Scottish and French cuisines; lunches (three courses for £16) offer the likes of red mullet with mussel veloute and pomme pureé.

Lian Pu

MAP P.48, POCKET MAP D6
14 Marshall St ☏ 0131 662 8895. Daily noon–10pm.

Thoroughly hip fast food restaurant among Edinburgh's surging Chinese student community, thanks to its true home-from-home cooking and palatable prices. Try the tofu noodle stir-fry for £6.70 with a side order of the deeply savoury spicy shredded cabbage.

Mosque Kitchen

MAP P.48, POCKET MAP F6
Edinburgh Central Mosque, 50 Potterrow (entrance on West Nicholson St)

The Grain Store restaurant

☎ 0131 629 1630. Daily 11.30am–8pm; closed Fri 12.50–1.50pm for prayer.
Out of the many "curry in a hurry" establishments that are cropping up around the Nicholson Street area, this is a true time-served veteran. Tagged onto the mosque, this no-nonsense canteen has for years been dishing out gloriously greasy, hugely filling plates of rice and curry for around £5.

Mother India's Cafe

MAP P.48, POCKET MAP D16
3–5 Infirmary St ☎ 0131 524 9801, ⓦ motherindiascafeedinburgh.co.uk.
Mon–Wed noon–2pm & 5–10.30pm, Thurs noon–10.30pm, Fri & Sat noon–11pm, Sun noon–10pm.
Tapas with a twist, so the restaurant slogan goes; the twist being that the food is Indian not Spanish. A novel concept, though the menu won't trouble seasoned curry connoisseurs, with classics like daal makhani and chicken tikka on offer (dishes £4–6).

No. Ten Restaurant

MAP P.48, POCKET MAP E17
10 Hill Place ☎ 0131 662 2080, ⓦ tenhill place.com. Daily 5–9.30pm.
Superb, award-winning, fine dining restaurant within the Ten Hill Place hotel. Begin with decadent chilled lobster bisque, tail and saffron mayo for £11 then waddle home after the pork loin, braised cheek and toffee apple.

The Piemaker

MAP P.48, POCKET MAP D15
38 South Bridge ☎ 0131 558 1728, ⓦ thepiemaker.co.uk. Mon–Wed 9am–8.15pm, Thurs & Fri 9am–10.45pm, Sat 10am–10.45pm, Sun 10.30am–7.45pm.
Possibly the cheapest place to fill up in town, with a mightily impressive range of pies from carnivore to vegan plus a few sweet ones. Prices hover around £2.50 each.

Spoon Café Bistro

MAP P.48, POCKET MAP D16
6a Nicholson St ☎ 0131 623 1752, ⓦ spoonedinburgh.co.uk. Mon–Sat 10am–10pm, Sun noon–5pm.
A homely, first-floor room with quirky, retro fittings serving reliably rustic two- and three-course menus with punchy flavours from £14. For late risers, the brunch menu is not to be missed with healthy fruit and yoghurt choices or decadent fry-ups. Under a different name, this was one of the cafés where J.K. Rowling first penned *Harry Potter* (the other being *The Elephant House* on George IV Bridge).

Tanjore

MAP P.48, POCKET MAP F6
6–8 Clerk St ☎ 0131 478 6518, ⓦ tanjore. co.uk. Mon–Fri noon–2.30pm & 5–10pm, Sat & Sun noon–3.30pm & 5–10pm.
South Indian cuisine's finest ambassador on these shores, drawing in all the regional standards including *vadai* (crunchy lentil doughnuts), *idli* (rice and lentil cake) and *sambar* – a distinctly rich, savoury curry with fragrant, bitter-sweet curry leaves. The freshly made *dosai* (lentil and rice crêpes) are among the lightest and crispiest you'll ever taste and come with a wide variety of fillings for around £7.

Tower Restaurant

MAP P.48, POCKET MAP C16
National Museum of Scotland, Chambers St ☎ 0131 225 3003, ⓦ tower-restaurant. com. Daily 10am–10pm.
Part of the museum complex and one of a handful of rooftop restaurants in town, this sophisticated space has fine views and sunsets northwest to the castle. The food is nonstop from brunch to dinner and is largely drawn from Scotland's own larder, with North Sea hake or Perthshire lamb mains for £32.

Pubs

Beehive Inn

MAP P.48, POCKET MAP B16
18–20 Grassmarket ☎ 0131 225 7171, ⓦ beehiveinn-edinburgh.co.uk.

Daily 11am–11pm.
One of the few family-friendly
pubs in the centre with an even
scarcer beer garden out back. Inside
it's a beautiful early Victorian
building with high-backed red
leather seating and corniced ceilings
in each of its three rooms.

Boteco Do Brasil

MAP P.48, POCKET MAP C16
47 Lothian St ☏ 0131 220 2487,
Ⓦ botecodobrasil.com. Daily 11am–3am.
Popular Brazilian themed bar with
a nonstop menu of street food
tapas and colourful cocktails. Look
out for live samba music sessions
or the salsa and bachata dance
lessons.

The Bow Bar

MAP P.48, POCKET MAP B15
80 West Bow ☏ 0131 226 7667, Ⓦ thebow
bar.co.uk. Mon–Sat noon–midnight, Sun
noon–11.30pm.
Wonderful old wood-panelled
bar and one of the nicest, most
convivial drinking spots in the
city centre, although it does get
uncomfortably busy at weekends.
Choose from among nearly 150
whiskies or a changing selection of
first-rate Scottish and English cask
beers.

The Brass Monkey

MAP P.48, POCKET MAP D16
14 Drummond St ☏ 0131 556 1961. Daily
noon–1am.
Popular boozer with students
thanks to its cheap drinks, regular
pub quizzes and daily 3pm film
screenings (free) in the cosy back
room.

Paradise Palms

MAP P.48. POCKET MAP D16
41 Lothian St ☏ 0131 225 4186, Ⓦ the
paradisepalms.com. Daily noon–3am.
In a location that has seen countless
bars come and go over the
decades, *Paradise Palms* has firmly
established itself as perhaps the
capital's most painfully hip outpost.
A tropical-thriftstore-cum-cabaret-

The Bow Bar

lounge theme, vegan and veggie
takes on Deep South soul food (like
the finger lickin' jackfruit nachos
for £7.50) and even a vinyl store
and electronica oriented record
label are all part of the appeal.

The Pear Tree

MAP P.48, POCKET MAP F6
38 West Nicolson St ☏ 0131 667 7533,
Ⓦ peartreeedinburgh.co.uk. Mon–Thurs
11am–midnight, Fri & Sat 11am–1am, Sun
noon–midnight.
Though this Edinburgh landmark
recently had its character all but
obliterated in a needless makeover,
the eighteenth-century exterior –
with two beautiful old pear trees
trained on its west wall – is still
a sight for sore eyes. Its greatest
asset has always been its large
cobbled courtyard – one of central
Edinburgh's very few bonafide
beer gardens, routinely rammed
come summer, with live bands
and barbecues.

Royal Oak

MAP P.48, POCKET MAP D16
1 Infirmary St ☏ 0131 557 2976,
Ⓦ royal-oak-folk.com. Mon–Sat
11.30am–2am, Sun 12.30pm–midnight.

Traditional Scottish pub hosting daily informal folk sessions performed by locals. On Sundays there's the "Wee Folk Club" (£5 entry) where they bring in soloists or groups from around the country and beyond.

Sandy Bell's

MAP P.48, POCKET MAP C16
25 Forrest Rd ☎ 0131 225 2751,
Ⓦ sandybellsedinburgh.co.uk. Sun–Fri noon–1am, Sat noon–midnight. Entry free.
A truly legendary, richly atmospheric and strictly traditional folk music bar that's been doing its thing since the 1940s. Famous for fine ales, malt whiskies and a good old sing-song, it's one of the last of its kind in the capital.

Under the Stairs

MAP P.48, POCKET MAP C16
3a Merchant St ☎ 0131 466 8550, Ⓦ under thestairs.org. Mon–Sat noon–1am, Sun noon–midnight.
Comfy, shabby-chic bar with great cocktails, popular with the pre-clubbing crowd. Food served late, with tasting boards (from £12.50 to £18.50) of cheese and oatcakes or charcuterie and pickles available right up until closing time.

Festival Theatre

Clubs and venues

Bannermans

MAP P.48, POCKET MAP D15
212 Cowgate ☎ 0131 556 3254,
Ⓦ bannermanslive.co.uk. Mon–Sat noon–1am, Sun 12.30pm–1am. Entry free–£8.
Another indefatigable grandaddy of Edinburgh's live music scene, with a labyrinth of caves and musky warrens located at the base of South Bridge. The most atmospheric joint in town in which to discover local indie bands hoping for a big break.

Bedlam Theatre

MAP P.48, POCKET MAP C16
11 Bristo Place ☎ 0131 629 0430,
Ⓦ bedlamtheatre.co.uk.
The oldest entirely student-run theatre in Britain, this deconsecrated neo-gothic church hosts over forty different performances annually.

The Bongo Club

MAP P.48, POCKET MAP C16
66 Cowgate ☎ 0131 558 8844, Ⓦ thebongo club.co.uk. Daily 11pm–3am, opens earlier on occasion. Entry £4–16.
Current home of this iconic, peripatetic Edinburgh club and arts venue; its line-up is routinely eclectic, experimental and always worth checking out. Though the legendary Four Corners is now sadly defunct, look out for the monthly grime and dubstep night Electrikal, funk and Latin fixture Soulsville (recently featuring a set from London-based Brazilian music legends, Mr Bongo – no relation!) and immortal reggae institution and "original roots advertiser", Messenger Sound System, which has outlasted (by decades!) almost every other club night in the city.

Festival Theatre

MAP P.48, POCKET MAP D16
13–29 Nicolson St ☎ 0131 529 6000,
Ⓦ edtheatres.com.
The largest stage in Britain, principally used for the Scottish

Opera and Scottish Ballet's appearances in the capital, but also for everything from cinematic festivals to Simon and Garfunkel.

The Jazz Bar

MAP P.48, POCKET MAP D16
1a Chambers St ☎ 0131 220 4298, ⓦ thejazzbar.co.uk. Mon–Fri 5pm–3am, Sat 1.30pm–3am, Sun 2pm–3am. Entry £4–14.
There's been a subterranean jazz bar on this site for decades, more or less. The current incarnation (set up by the late jazz drummer Bill Kyle in 2005) hosts up to five performances a day, every day, with an eclectic roster and a generous definition of jazz seeing soul, funk, blues and electronica all getting a look-in. All door money (usually around £4) goes directly to the musicians.

La Belle Angele

MAP P.48, POCKET MAP D15
11 Hasties Close, Cowgate ☎ 0131 225 8382, ⓦ la-belleangele.com. Club nights 10pm–3am. Entry free.
A legendary 90s venue which recently rose from the ashes, quite literally, after it was burned to the ground in a 2002 fire. Radiohead, Oasis and some of the city's best club nights graced it back in the day. In its new incarnation, the likes of Craig Charles and Leftfield have shown up for DJ sets, while midweek bass frenzy Loco Kamanchi is one of the most credible student nights around.

The Liquid Room

MAP P.48, POCKET MAP B15
9c Victoria St ☎ 0131 225 2564, ⓦ liquid room.com. Regular club nights Fri & Sat 10.30pm–3am. Club night entry £4–7.
Another club and live music venue with a long and chequered history that has, in its time, played host to luminaries as diverse as Mogwai, John Martyn, Kelis, The Beta Band, Grandmaster Flash, Nancy Sinatra and Franz Ferdinand. These days they're home to indie superclub franchise Propaganda, a fair dose

of tribute bands and the occasional cutting edge touring act such as Sleaford Mods, while cult club/art night Rhythm Machine recently moved into The Warehouse annex.

Mash House

MAP P.48, POCKET MAP D15
37 Guthrie St (entrance up Hastie's Close from the Cowgate) ☎ 0131 220 2514, ⓦ themashhouse.co.uk. Club nights 10pm–3am. Entry £2–12.
Sequestered away in a side street hidey-hole just off the Cowgate, this is regarded one of the best venues in the city among bands, promoters, DJs and punters, and has hosted the likes of Andrew Weatherall. The downstairs dancefloor is just the right size for working up a sweat, especially when Samedia are in town (usually first Fri of month) with their trademark blend of tropical bass.

Sneaky Pete's

MAP P.48, POCKET MAP C16
73 Cowgate ☎ 0131 225 1757, ⓦ sneaky petes.co.uk. Daily 11pm–3am. Entry £2–3.
Condensed sweat and a fiercely eclectic roster characterise this 100-capacity Cowgate perennial, often cited as the soul of the capital's grassroots scene. Club nights such as Wasabi Disco and Teesh are solid fixtures, while the tiny stage has hosted everyone from seminal DJ Bill Brewster to veteran Japanese psyche-rockers Acid Mothers Temple.

Wee Red Bar

MAP P.48, POCKET MAP B16
Edinburgh Art College, Lauriston Place ☎ 0131 651 5859, ⓦ weeredbar.co.uk. Club nights 10.30/11pm–3am. Entry £3–15.
This art college legend may be small but its history is long: monthly club night The Egg is to indie music what the Bongo's Messenger (see page 56) is to reggae. Also one of the few places in the capital to cater to northern soul, with the likes of Keb Darge having pitched up in the past.

Holyrood and Arthur's Seat

At the foot of Canongate lies Holyrood, for centuries known as Edinburgh's royal quarter, with its ruined thirteenth-century abbey and the Palace of Holyroodhouse. Over the last few decades, however, the area has been transformed by the addition of Enric Miralles' highly controversial Scottish Parliament, a love-it or loathe-it concrete monolith "almost surging out of the rock" – as Miralles put it – of adjacent Arthur's Seat. This extinct volcano remains the centrepiece of Holyrood Park, a natural wilderness in the very heart of the modern city comprising a stunning variety of landscapes. Incredibly for a major European capital, you can sit in the lee of Arthur's Seat, in the centre of the glen, and not see a single high rise nor indeed any trace of urban life.

The Palace of Holyroodhouse

MAP P.60, POCKET MAP G14
Canongate ☎ 0303 123 7306, ⊛ royal collection.org.uk/visit/palace-of-holyroodhouse. Daily: April–Oct 9.30am–6pm; Nov–March 9.30am–4.30pm; last admission 1hr 30min before closing (palace is closed to visitors when the Queen is in residence; check the website for advance notice). £12.50 or £17.50 for joint entry with Queen's Gallery; includes an audio tour.
In its present form, the **Palace of Holyroodhouse** is largely a seventeenth-century creation, planned for Charles II. However, the tower house of the old palace (the sole survivor of a fire during Oliver Cromwell's occupation) built for James V in 1532 was skilfully incorporated to form the northwestern block of today's building, with a virtual mirror image of it erected as a counterbalance at the other end.

Tours of the palace move through a series of royal **reception rooms** featuring some outstanding encrusted plasterwork, each more impressive than the last, an idea Charles II had picked up from his cousin Louis XIV's Versailles. On the northern side of the internal quadrangle, the **Great Gallery** extends almost the full length of the palace and is dominated by portraits of 96 Scottish kings, painted by Jacob de Wet in 1684 to illustrate the lineage of Stewart royalty.

As you move into the oldest part of the palace, known as **James V's tower**, the formal, ceremonial tone gives way to dark medieval history, with a tight spiral staircase leading to the chambers used by **Mary, Queen of Scots**. These contain various relics, though the most compelling viewing is a tiny supper room, from where in 1566 Mary's Italian secretary, **David Rizzio**, was dragged by conspirators, who included her jealous husband, Lord Darnley, to the outer chamber and stabbed 56 times.

Holyrood Abbey

MAP P.60, POCKET MAP G14
⊛ historicenvironment.scot/visit-a-place/places/holyrood-abbey. Free tour included in palace ticket on a "turn-up-and-go" basis; £21.50 for joint Palace of Holyroodhouse and Queen's Gallery ticket which also includes history tour of formal palace gardens (May–Sept only).
Standing beside the palace are the evocative ruins of **Holyrood**

Abbey, some of which date back to the thirteenth century. Gutted in 1688 by an anti-Catholic mob, the roof finally tumbled down in 1768. The melancholy scene inspired Felix Mendelssohn, who in 1829 wrote: "Everything is in ruins and mouldering … I believe I have found the beginning of my Scottish Symphony there today." Adjacent to the abbey are the formal palace gardens, open to visitors during the summer months. Plans are afoot to recreate both the palace's pioneering, seventeenth-century **physic garden** (the original cue for Edinburgh's Royal Botanic Garden) and a flowering meadow inspired by the abbey's fifteenth-century monastic garden.

Queen's Gallery

MAP P.60, POCKET MAP G14
Canongate ☎ 0303 123 7306, ⓦ royal collection.org.uk/visit/the-queens-gallery-palace-of-holyroodhouse. Daily: April–Oct 9.30am–6pm; Nov–March 9.30am–4.30pm, last admission 1hr before closing. £7 or £17.50 for joint entry with Palace of Holyroodhouse; includes an audio tour.

The ruins of Holyrood Abbey

Essentially an adjunct to the Palace of Holyroodhouse, the **Queen's Gallery** is located in a former church directly between the palace and the Scottish Parliament. With just two principal viewing rooms, it's a compact space, but has an appealing contemporary style. It's used to display changing exhibitions from the **Royal Collection**, a vast array of art treasures held by the Queen on behalf of the British nation. Recent displays have included the seminal butterfly studies of German botanical artist and entomologist, Maria Merian, conceived in Suriname at the turn of the eighteenth century.

The Scottish Parliament

MAP P.60, POCKET MAP G14
Horse Wynd ☎ 0800 092 7600, ⓦ visitparliament.scot. Mon, Fri & Sat 10am–5pm (last entry 4.30pm), Tues–Thurs 9am–6.30pm (last entry 6pm). Free guided tours (1hr); booking is recommended (access is limited to lobby and debating chamber if unguided). Free crèche.
The most controversial public building to be erected in Scotland since World War II, the **Scottish**

Garden Lobby, Scottish Parliament

Parliament houses the country's directly elected assembly, which re-convened in 1999 for the first time in almost 300 years (see page 151). Anvil-shaped panels clad the exterior and the extraordinary windows of the offices are shaped like the profile of a mountain or a section of the Forth Rail Bridge. While the stark concrete interior makes it look unfinished, there are moments where grace and boldness convene, exemplified by the **Garden Lobby**, with a fascinating roof of glass panels forming the shape of an upturned boat.

There's free access into the building's **entrance lobby**, where you'll find a small exhibition providing some historical, political and architectural background. If Parliament is in session, it's normally possible to watch proceedings in the **debating chamber** from the public gallery, though you have

Holyrood and Arthur's Seat

RESTALRIG

LONDON ROAD
CALTON
MARIONVILLE ROAD
RESTALRIG AVENUE
CRAIGENTINNY AVE

MEADOWBANK
LONDON ROAD

Regent
Gardens
Ingleby
Gallery
SPRING GARDENS
Piershill
Cemetery

Regent Road
NORTHFIELD

ABBEYHILL

Palace of
Holyroodhouse
QUEEN'S DRIVE
St Margaret's
Loch
PAISLEY CRES.

CANONGATE
Scottish
Parliament
QUEEN'S DRIVE

WILLOWBRAE ROAD

SEE INSET MAP

Holyrood Park
MEADOW-
FIELD

QUEEN'S DRIVE
Dunsapie
Loch
Meadowfield
Park
MEADOWFIELD DRIVE

Salisbury Crags
Arthur's
Seat
▲ (823ft)
DUDDINGSTON

QUEEN'S DRIVE
OLD CHURCH LANE

HOLYROOD PK RD
Duddingston
Kirk
Dr Neil's
Garden

University of
Edinburgh
Pollock Halls
of Residence
DUDDINGSTON LOW ROAD
Duddingston
Loch

DALKEITH ROAD
THE INNOCENT RAILWAY PATH

NEWINGTON
PRIESTFIELD ROAD
Prestonfield
House

to get a pass from the front desk in the lobby. To see the rest of the interior properly you'll need to join one of the highly recommended **regular guided tours**. Special tours dedicated to the architecture of the building and its collection of contemporary Scottish art also take place, albeit much less frequently – check the website for details.

Dynamic Earth

MAP P.60, POCKET MAP G15
112 Holyrood Rd ☏ 0131 550 7800,
ⓦ dynamicearth.co.uk. April–Oct daily 10am–5.30pm; July & Aug daily 10am–6pm; Nov–March Wed–Sun 10am–5.30pm; last entry 1hr 30min before closing. Adults £15, under-15s £9.50 (online tickets £13.50/£8.55).

Beneath a pincushion of white metal struts that make it look like a miniature version of London's Millennium Dome, **Dynamic Earth** is a hi-tech, immersive attraction based on the wonders of the natural world and aimed at families with kids between 5 and 15. **Galleries** cover the formation of the earth and continents with crashing sound effects and a shaking floor, while the calmer grandeur of glaciers and oceans is explored through magnificent large-screen landscape footage. Further on, the polar regions – complete with a real iceberg – and tropical jungles are imaginatively re-created, with interactive computer screens and special effects at every turn.

Relief for scienced-out parents is at hand via the occasional **Dome Nights** event (check website for upcoming shows), with the venue recently hosting a Fringe-partnered dad-rock extravaganza in the shape of Pink Floyd's *Dark Side of the Moon* beamed around the dome in its entirety, complete with obligatory cosmic visuals.

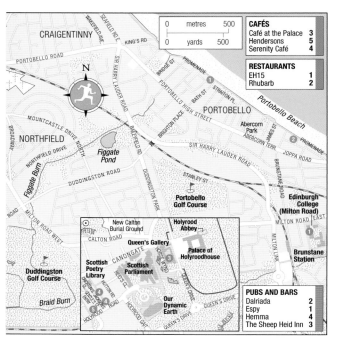

The Radical Road

In a city of conspicuously royalist street names, **The Radical Road**, high up on Salisbury Crags (see page 62), stands defiantly apart, the name deriving from the **Radical War** of 1820, in which Glaswegian weavers rose up against social injustice and exploitation. Inevitably, the rebellion was mercilessly crushed and its leaders hung. Ever eager to do his bit for king and country, **Walter Scott** subsequently suggested that the jobless weavers be put to work paving a path through the Crags, their political sympathies ultimately christening their toil.

Holyrood Park

Comprising a dazzling array of landscapes – hills, crags, moorland, marshes, glens, lochs and fields – packed into 650 acres, **Holyrood Park** is Scotland in miniature. Once a royal hunting estate, it was given park status in the sixteenth century by King James V. While old photographs of the park show crops growing and sheep grazing, it's now used mostly by outdoor enthusiasts. A single tarred road, **Queen's Drive**, loops through the park, perfect for a circular cycle route.

Salisbury Crags

The sheer cliff face of **Salisbury Crags** is one of Edinburgh's most formidable natural features, climbing high above the Canongate and offering up an unforgettable view of Edinburgh, the Pentland Hills and

Arthur's Seat

fringes of Fife, especially at sunset. An easy hour-long circular route begins across from Holyroodhouse; a path called "The Radical Road" (see page 62) winds southwards across the crags for a little under a mile before you have the opportunity to hike north through the glen separating them from Arthur's Seat and back to your starting point.

Arthur's Seat

The usual starting point for the ascent of **Arthur's Seat**, which at 823ft above sea level towers over Edinburgh's numerous high points, is just across from the car park at Holyrood Palace, or – if you're driving – from the car park at Dunsapie Loch. Part of a volcano which last saw action 350 million years ago, its connections to the legendary king are fairly sketchy: the name is likely to be a corruption of the Gaelic *Ard-na-said*, or "height of arrows". From the Palace it's a 30–40min walk/climb up grassy slopes to the rocky summit. With clear weather, views might just stretch to the English border and the Atlantic Ocean. While the summit can get very crowded, there are any number of quiet trails snaking all over the lower hills – don't be afraid to get off the beaten path and explore.

Duddingston Village

The beguiling conservation village of **Duddingston**, below the southeastern flanks of Arthur's Seat some 2.5 miles from the city centre, is attractively set on the

Duddingston Loch

shores of **Duddingston Loch** – best known as the setting for Henry Raeburn's *Reverend Robert Walker Skating on Duddingston Loch*, on show at the National Gallery (see page 70). Most visitors come here for a stiff drink at the historic *Sheep Heid Inn* (see page 65) after hiking down from Arthur's Seat, and there's no more appealing place to escape the city's bustle. A plaque on the handsome (private) house at no.8–10 The Causeway, records it as the site of **Bonnie Prince Charlie's Council of War** prior to his routing of government troops at the Battle of Prestonpans in September 1745.

Dr Neil's Garden

MAP P.60
Old Church Lane ☏ 07849 187 995,
ⓦ drneilsgarden.co.uk. Garden daily 10am–dusk. Free (donation welcome). Bus #42.
Completely secluded behind the twelfth-century Duddingston Kirk, and accessed via a gate in the high stone walls of Old Church Lane is **Dr Neil's Garden**, one of Edinburgh's – and perhaps one of Scotland's – best kept secrets. This truly special place comprises a lattice of cobbled paths, stone benches and contemplative nooks and crannies, bordered by hardy shrubs and alpine flowers, and shaded by musky Scots pine punctuated with rarities like North America sequoia and Chilean araucaria (monkey puzzle), all sloping down to ravishing views of Duddingston Loch and its rich birdlife. Created out of rocky grazing land over just a few decades by a husband and wife team of GPs, the garden fulfilled a dual function of recreation and healing, with their patients encouraged to tend it and partake of the tranquil air. Even today, it places an emphasis on wellbeing and welcomes volunteers.

Portobello

Among Edinburgh's least expected assets is its **beach**, a mile-long stretch of golden sand, most of which falls within **Portobello**, or "Porty", in local parlance, a suburb around three miles east of the centre of town (bus #15 or #26 eastbound from Princes St). As well as a fiercely independent and community-minded spirit, it retains a certain wind-bleached charm thanks to some attractive Victorian buildings and its delightful promenade. On hot summer weekends the beach can be a mass of swimmers, sunbathers, surfers and pleasure boats.

Cafés

Café at the Palace

MAP P.60, POCKET MAP G14
Canongate ⓦ royalcollection.org.uk.
Daily: April–Oct 9.30am–6pm; Nov–March
9.30am–4.30pm; afternoon tea served
daily 1–4pm.

The rarefied setting of the glass-roofed Palace Mews and Courtyard at Holyroodhouse makes for a suitably genteel backdrop to a classic afternoon tea (£18.95), served in specially commissioned china; if you're feeling particularly regal, treat yourself to the champagne option (£27).

Hendersons

MAP P.60, POCKET MAP F15
Holyrood Road ⓣ 0131 557 1606,
ⓦ hendersonsofedinburgh.co.uk/locations/
holyrood. Mon–Sat 7.30am–5pm, Sun
10am–4pm.

The newest addition to the portfolio of Edinburgh's veteran vegetarian and vegan institution, attracting office workers and tourists for meat-free sandwiches, wraps and mains, as well as creative veggie takes on street food staples.

Café at the Palace

Serenity Café

MAP P.60, POCKET MAP F14
8 Jacksons Entry. Daily 9am–5pm.

Snug between the Canongate and Holyrood Road, this pioneering community café was the first of its kind when it opened in 2009, set up and run by recovering addicts, with all profits ploughed back into helping others. A uniquely welcoming vibe and delicious, great value food (mains under a fiver) has since made it a favourite with both locals and ethically minded visitors.

Restaurants

EH15

MAP P.60
The Club, 24 Milton Road East, Portobello
ⓣ 0131 344 7344, ⓦ theclubedinburgh.
com/eh15-restaurant-bar. Sittings Tues–
Thurs noon–12.45pm & 6.15–6.45pm, Fri
12.15–12.45pm.

Gourmet grub on a budget as college catering students test their culinary mettle – the evening Masterchef Menu is a real bargain at £10. Inevitably hit-and-miss but chances are you'll eat like a food critic for the price of a takeaway,

Café at the Palace

and the wraparound, fifth-floor views are sensational.

Rhubarb

MAP P.60
Prestonfield House, Priestfield Rd ☎ 0131 225 7800, ⓦ prestonfield.com/dine/rhubarb. Mon–Sat noon–2pm & 6–10pm, Sun 12.30–3pm & 6–10pm.
Ensconced in glorious pastoral isolation among the red and gold floral riot of A-listed *Prestonfield House* hotel, this place is tailor-made for a lavish romantic dinner (mains generally £20–40). Locally sourced and gourmet the food may be, but they're not above a humble plate of rhubarb crumble and custard either, Prestonfield Estate being the first in Scotland to grow the stuff.

Pubs

Dalriada

MAP P.60
Promenade, Portobello ☎ 0131 454 4500, ⓦ dalriadabar.co.uk. Mon–Wed 2–11pm, Thurs 2pm–midnight, Fri 2pm–1am, Sat noon–1am, Sun 12.30–11pm.
"Edinburgh's Bar on the Beach" is housed in a turreted Victorian pile on Portobello's Promenade, enjoying glorious sea views. Craft beers are on tap, while a huge bay window and a roaring fire set the scene for live folk and world music sessions (Wed–Sat).

The Espy

MAP P.60
62–64 Bath Street, Portobello ☎ 0131 669 0082, ⓦ bit.ly/the-espy. Daily 9am–1am.
Hugely popular Porty bar, crammed with kitsch and beloved of locals (and their dogs), beachcombers and families, and serving up a full menu of fairly typical bar food, as well as cocktails and milkshakes.

Hemma

MAP P.60, POCKET MAP F15
Tunbuilding, 73 Holyrood Road ☎ 0131 629 3327, ⓦ bodabar.com/hemma. Mon 11am–8pm, Tues & Wed 11am–9pm (till

The Sheep Heid Inn

11pm April–Sept), Thurs 11am–midnight, Fri & Sat 11am–1am, Sun 10am–8pm.
Plate-glass brutalism meets shabby Scandi chic at family-friendly *Hemma*. Sip a cocktail in one of their mismatched chairs, tuck into pickled herring (£7) or share a genuine, non-metaphorical smörgåsbord (£11).

The Sheep Heid Inn

MAP P.60
43–45 The Causeway, Duddingston ☎ 0131 661 7974, ⓦ thesheepheidedinburgh.co.uk. Mon–Thurs 11am–11pm, Fri & Sat 11am–midnight, Sun noon–11pm; food served Mon–Sat noon–10pm, Sun 12.30–9.30pm.
Scotland's oldest – and possibly most famous – pub and one-time watering hole to, variously, Mary Queen of Scots, King James VI and Bonnie Prince Charlie, the *Sheep Heid* is said to have first opened its doors in 1360. This impeccable historical pedigree is complemented by a charming courtyard, a nineteenth-century skittle alley and a menu of reasonable gastro-grub (mains generally £10–15). The Queen herself left locals gobsmacked when she turned up out of the blue for a meal in 2016, eating out in public being something she rarely does.

Princes Street

Running parallel to and north of the historic Royal Mile, Edinburgh's principle shopping thoroughfare, Princes Street, must surely rank as one of the most picturesque in the world. Its mile long stretch of High Street chain stores that occupy only the north side of the street face out to the jagged silhouette of the Old Town and castle, while to the east views open up to the 200ft Scott Monument, the late Victorian Balmoral Hotel and beyond to the extinct volcanoes of Calton Hill and Arthur's Seat. Originally a residential street named in honour of King George IV's sons, few of Princes Street's original buildings survive; displaced by the medley of retail outlets that sprung up during the Victorian era and beyond. Luckily the delightful residents' gardens across the street were retained and opened to the public.

General Register House

MAP P.68, POCKET MAP C13
2 Princes St ☎ 0131 535 1314,
Ⓦ nrscotland.gov.uk. Free with a Reader's ticket. Mon–Fri 9am–4.30pm.
Designed in 1774 by Robert Adam, the **General Register House** is the most distinguished building on Princes Street. Today it's home to the **Scotland's People Centre**, a dedicated family history unit which acts as a single point of access for those researching genealogical records. To visit you will need to bring two forms of ID and two passport sized

General Register House on Princes Street

photographs in order to obtain a free Reader's ticket. Once that's out of the way, you can pore over a mixed archive of records ranging from national censuses, criminal records and, stretching back to 1553, old parish registers of births, marriages and deaths. A large database complements the physical records and there are a number of computers for public use if you don't have your own. Part of the appeal of embarking on some research is the opportunity to spend time in the elegant interior, centred on a glorious rotunda, lavishly decorated with plasterwork and antique-style medallions.

Balmoral Hotel

MAP P.68, POCKET MAP C14
1 Princes St ☎ 0131 556 2414,
Ⓦ roccofortehotels.com.

A time capsule of late Victorian splendour, the massive baronial style building and clock tower standing proud at Princes Street's east end is one of Edinburgh's most iconic landmarks. The city's most luxurious hotel, the **Balmoral** – meaning 'majestic dwelling' in Gaelic – boasts a Michelin starred restaurant, a pool, spa and suites that can set you back as much as £1800 a night. The final Harry Potter book, *The Deathly Hallows* was famously penned in room 552, since renamed the 'J.K. Rowling Suite'. Outside, the clock tower faithfully tells the wrong time; it's been set three minutes fast since 1902 to help passengers catch their trains on time at the station below.

The Edinburgh Dungeon

MAP P.68, POCKET MAP C14
31 Market St ☎ 0871 423 2550,
Ⓦ thedungeons.com/edinburgh. Opening times vary daily but generally open daily 11am–5pm. Adult £18, child £14 (£13 and £11 respectively if bought online)

Edinburgh's tourist industry gets decent mileage from the villains and ghosts of the city's mediaeval past but none more so

Balmoral Hotel

than the **Edinburgh Dungeon**. This family-friendly attraction puts on a theatrical guided tour of subterranean chambers that include a torture room, an anatomy theatre and plenty of stories of old Edinburgh with accompanying special effects as well as couple of joyfully macabre rides.

The Fruitmarket Gallery

MAP P.68, POCKET MAP C14
45 Market St ☎ 0131 225 2383,
Ⓦ fruitmarket.co.uk. Daily 10am–6pm. Free.

This reputable contemporary art gallery has been exhibiting cutting edge national and international artists' work since it took over the city's former fruit and veg market building in the 1970s. There's no permanent collection at the **Fruitmarket Gallery**; just a changing series of innovative displays that have previously included work from the late, influential sculpture artist, Louise Bourgeois and a slightly sinister study of self and symmetry by Mark Wallinger.

Also within the gallery building is a small bookshop selling art,

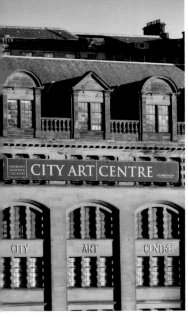

City Art Centre

design, photography and children's titles as well as an excellent café (see page 74).

City Art Centre

MAP P.68, POCKET MAP C14
2 Market St ☎ 0131 529 3993,
🌐 edinburghmuseums.org.uk. Wed–Sat 10am–5pm, Sun noon–5pm. Free.
Home to probably the most diverse body of post sixteenth-century Scottish art in the world, the **City Art Centre**'s collection represents every national movement from the post-impressionist Glasgow Boys to the Colourists of the early 1900s. Particularly interesting from a historical perspective is the gallery's scenescape collection of Edinburgh's streets and markets that stretches back as far as the 16th century.

The gallery's six floors are also used to display a wide range of temporary exhibits that have included the original Star

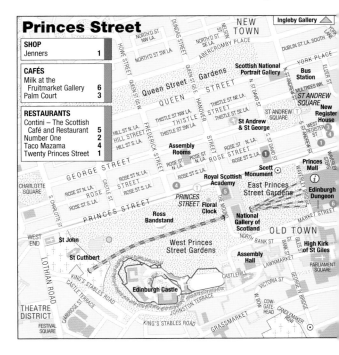

Wars costumes and a sculpture compilation from the late 70s and 80s.

Princes Street Gardens

MAP P.68, POCKET MAP B14

☎ 0131 529 7921. Daily 7am–10pm. Free.

It's hard to imagine that the **Princes Street Gardens**, which flank nearly the entire length of Princes Street, were once the stagnant, foul-smelling Nor' Loch into which the effluent of the Old Town flowed for centuries. The railway has since replaced the water and today a sunken cutting carries the main lines out of Waverley Station to the west and north. The gardens, split into east and west sections, were originally the private domain of Princes Street residents and their well-placed acquaintances, only becoming a public park in 1876. These days, the swathes of green lawn, colourful flower beds and mature trees are a green lung for the city centre: on sunny days local office workers appear in their droves at lunchtime, while in the run-up to Christmas the gardens' eastern section is home to a German Market, a towering Ferris wheel and a number of other appealingly lit rides. The larger and more verdant western section has the world's first floral clock from 1903 and the Ross Bandstand, a popular but tired looking Festival venue that is braced for demolition and replacement with an intriguing earth sheltered structure, fittingly dubbed the "Hobbit-House" for its undulating roof and arched frontage. Cross the nearby footbridge over the railway tracks and the gardens diverge east along the lush slopes below the castle's esplanade and west, swinging around the castle's precipitous flank up towards the **Old Town**.

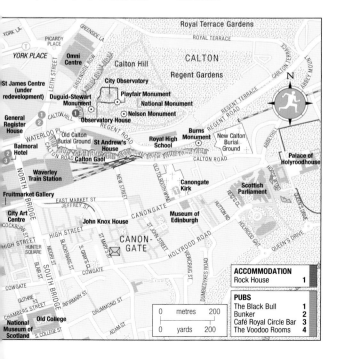

ACCOMMODATION
Rock House   1

PUBS
The Black Bull   1
Bunker   2
Café Royal Circle Bar   3
The Voodoo Rooms   4

Scott Monument

Scott Monument

MAP P.68, POCKET MAP C14
East Princes Street Gardens ☏ 0131 529
4068, ⓦ edinburghmuseums.org.uk. April–
Sept daily 10am–7pm; Oct–March daily
10am–4pm. £5.

Facing the Victorian shopping
emporium Jenners, and set within
East Princes Street Gardens, the
200ft-high **Scott Monument**
was erected in memory of prolific
author and patriot Sir Walter Scott
within a few years of his death. The
largest monument in the world to
a man of letters, the architecture is
closely modelled on Scott's beloved
Melrose Abbey (see page 126),
and the rich sculptural decoration
shows sixteen Scottish writers
and sixty-four characters from
Scott's famous *Waverley* novels.
On the central plinth at the base
of the monument is a **statue** of
Scott with his deerhound Maida,
carved from a thirty-ton block of
Carrara marble.

Inside, a tightly winding spiral
staircase climbs 287 steps to a
narrow platform near the top: from
here, you can enjoy some inspiring
– if vertiginous – vistas of the city
below and hills and firths beyond.

National Gallery of Scotland

MAP P.68, POCKET MAP B14
The Mound, Princes St ☏ 0131 624 6200,
ⓦ nationalgalleries.org. Fri–Wed 10am–
5pm, Thurs 10am–7pm. Free; entrance
charge for some temporary exhibitions.

Built as a "temple to the fine arts"
in 1850, the **National Gallery of
Scotland** houses Scotland's premier
collection of pre-twentieth-century
European art in the larger of two
grand Neoclassical buildings found
at the foot of the Mound.

Though by no means as vast as
national collections found elsewhere
in Europe, it does include a clutch
of exquisite old masters and some
superb Impressionist works.
Benefiting greatly from being a
manageable size, its series of elegant
octagonal rooms is enlivened
by imaginative displays and a
pleasantly unrushed atmosphere.

On the ground floor the rooms
have been restored to their 1850s
appearance, with pictures hung
closely together on claret-coloured
walls, often on two levels, and
intermingled with sculptures
and objets d'art to produce a
deliberately cluttered effect. As a
result some lesser works, which

would otherwise languish in the vaults, are on display, a good 15ft up. The **layout** is broadly chronological, starting in the upper rooms above the gallery's entrance on the Mound and continuing clockwise around the ground floor.

Among the Gallery's most valuable treasures are **Hugo van der Goes'** *Trinity Panels*, on a long-term loan from the Queen. Painted in the mid-fifteenth century, they were commissioned by Provost Edward Bonkil for the Holy Trinity Collegiate Church, which was later demolished to make way for Edinburgh's Waverley Station. Bonkil can be seen amid the company of organ-playing angels in the best preserved of the four panels, while on the reverse sides are portraits of James III, his son (the future James IV) and Queen Margaret of Denmark. The panels are turned by the gallery staff regularly.

Elsewhere proudly displayed in their own room, Poussin's Seven Sacraments series marks the first attempt to portray scenes from the life of Jesus realistically, rather than through images dictated by artistic conventions.

Among the canvases by **Rembrandt** are a poignant *Self-Portrait Aged 51* and the suggestive *Woman in Bed*, which is thought to represent the biblical figure of Sarah on her wedding night, waiting for her husband Tobias to put the devil to flight.

Among the gallery's Scottish contingent and one of the most popular portraits is the immediately recognizable painting of a lesser-known pastor, *Reverend Robert Walker Skating on Duddingston Loch*, by **Henry Raeburn.**

Royal Scottish Academy

MAP P.68, POCKET MAP B14
The Mound ☎ 0131 225 6671,
ⓦ royalscottishacademy.org. Mon–Sat
10am–5pm, Sun noon–5pm. Free; entrance
charge for some temporary exhibitions.

Based in the impressive Grecian building at the foot of the Mound, the **Royal Scottish Academy** was founded in 1826 as a unique independent body with a remit to promote contemporary Scottish art through exhibitions, scholarship administration and residencies. Its archive of well over a thousand canvases and architectural works stretching back to the eighteenth century is considered a "Recognised Collection of National Significance" by Museum Galleries Scotland.

The exhibitions broadly focus on the modern however, as the very best of the nation's emerging and established talent get a rare opportunity to display their wares in a prestigious gallery. If you see something you like it might be possible to take it home. Many of the displays are for sale, although the prices are generally out of reach of most people.

Calton Hill

MAP P.68, POCKET MAP E13
Always open.
Edinburgh's enduring tag as the "Athens of the North" is nowhere better earned than on **Calton Hill**,

Calton Hill

PRINCES STREET

the volcanic crag which rises up above the eastern end of Princes Street. Numerous architects homed in on it as a showcase for their most ambitious and grandiose buildings and monuments, the presence of which emphasizes Calton's aloof air and sense of detachment. It's also one of the best viewpoints from which to appreciate the city as a whole, with its tightly knitted suburbs, landmark Old and New Town buildings and the Firth of Forth beyond.

Calton Gaol

MAP P.68, POCKET MAP D13
Waterloo Place. No public access.

Many visitors arriving into Waverley Station at Calton Hill's southern drop imagine the picturesque castellated building hard up against the rock to be Edinburgh Castle itself. In fact, it's the only surviving part of the **Calton Gaol**, once Edinburgh's main prison where former serial killer William Burke spent his final hours before being

executed on Lawnmarket. Most of the prison was demolished in the 1930s to make way for the looming Art Deco St Andrew's House, which is today occupied by civil servants. The door to the cell of the condemned was reclaimed and can now be seen in the *Beehive Inn* (see page 54).

Old Calton Burial Ground

MAP P.68, POCKET MAP D13
Waterloo Place. Open 24hr. Free.

On Calton Hill's southern slopes, tucked behind a line of high, dark, forbidding walls, the picturesque assembly of mausoleums and gravestones of **Old Calton Burial Ground**, some at a jaunty angle and others weathered with age, makes for an absorbing wander. Notable among the monuments are the cylindrical memorial by Robert Adam to the philosopher David Hume, one of Edinburgh's greatest sons, and a piercing obelisk commemorating various political martyrs.

Gravestones in Old Calton Burial Ground

Nelson Monument

MAP P.68, POCKET MAP E13
Summit of Calton Hill ☏ 0131 556 2716,
ⓦ edinburghmuseums.org.uk. April–Sept
Mon–Sat 10am–7pm, Sun noon–5pm; Oct–
March Mon–Sat 10am–4pm. £5.

Robert Louis Stevenson reckoned
that Calton Hill was the best place
to view Edinburgh, "since you
can see the Castle, which you lose
from the Castle, and Arthur's Seat,
which you cannot see from Arthur's
Seat". Though the panoramas
from ground level are spectacular
enough, those from the top of
the **Nelson Monument**, perched
near the summit of Calton Hill,
are even better. Each day at 1pm
a white ball drops down a mast at
the top of the monument; this,
together with the one o'clock gun
fired from the Castle battlements,
once provided a daily check for
the mariners of Leith, who needed
accurate chronometers to ensure
reliable navigation at sea.

National Monument

MAP P.68, POCKET MAP E13
Summit of Calton Hill. Always open.

The **National Monument** is
often referred to as "Edinburgh's
Disgrace", yet many locals admire
this unfinished and somewhat
ungainly attempt to replicate the
Parthenon atop Calton Hill. Begun
in 1826 as a memorial to the dead of
the Napoleonic Wars, the project's
shortage of funds led architect
William Playfair to ensure that
even with just twelve of the massive
columns completed, the folly would
still serve as a striking landmark.

City Observatory

MAP P.68, POCKET MAP E13
Summit of Calton Hill. Closed for
redevelopment; due to open in 2018.

Designed by William Playfair in
1818, the **City Observatory** is
the largest of the buildings at the
summit of Calton Hill although
because of pollution and the advent
of street lighting, which impaired
views of the stars, the observatory

The National Monument on Calton Hill

proper had to be relocated to
Blackford Hill (see page 116)
before the end of the nineteenth
century. At the time of writing,
works are ongoing to turn the
building into a contemporary art
gallery and restaurant complex.

At the corner of the curtain
walls is the castellated Observatory
House, one of the few surviving
buildings by James Craig, designer
of the New Town.

Ingleby Gallery

MAP P.68, POCKET MAP E3
33 Barony Street ☏ 0131 556 4441,
ⓦ inglebygallery.com. Wed–Sat
11am–5pm.

Set unexpectedly among the
grand residential houses of this
prestigious Georgian street to the
east of Calton Hill, the **Ingleby
Gallery** is a highly reputable
exhibition space that attracts the
work of little known artists from
around the world. Recent displays
have included eccentric Antiguan
painter, sculpturist and writer
Frank Walter whose works have
included Hitler playing cricket and
Charles and Diana portrayed as
Adam and Eve.

Shop

Jenners

MAP P.68, POCKET MAP B14

48 Princes St ☎ 0344 800 3725, ⓦ houseof
fraser.co.uk. Mon–Wed 9.30am–6.30pm,
Thurs 9.30am–8pm, Fri 9.30am–7pm, Sat
9am–7pm, Sun 11am–6pm.

Edinburgh's venerable department
store is a true Victorian delight
outside and in. The current
building originally opened in 1895
and introduced many technical
innovations including hydraulic
lifts and electric lights. Today the
top brands in fashion and perfume
take up the majority of its five floors
although it has cafés, a food shop
and a department run by London's
famous toy sellers, Hamley's.

Cafés

Milk at the Fruitmarket Gallery

MAP P.68, POCKET MAP C14

45 Market St ☎ 0131 226 8195,
ⓦ fruitmarket.co.uk. Daily 10am–6pm.

This attractive café feels like an
extension of the gallery space, its
airy, reflective ambience enhanced by

Contini at the National Gallery

the wall of glass onto the street. Lots
of colourful, modern and healthy
brunch options are served here, like
avocado and za'atar with poached
egg on toast for £5.75. Artisan cakes
and expensive coffee too.

Palm Court

MAP P.68, POCKET MAP C14

The Balmoral Hotel, 1 Princes St ☎ 0131
556 2414, ⓦ roccofortehotels.com.
Afternoon tea noon–5pm.

The ultimate afternoon tea
experience; within the Balmoral
Hotel complex the oval-shaped
Palm Court, with its glass cupola,
Grecian pillars and tall potted
palms, has somehow struck a
balance between decadence and
tasteful understatement. Try the
hotel's signature tea blend with the
exquisite hand made pastries while
a harpist recites from the balcony.
Afternoon tea £37.50.

Restaurants

Contini – The Scottish Café and Restaurant

MAP P.68, POCKET MAP B14

National Gallery of Scotland, The Mound
☎ 0131 225 1550, ⓦ contini.com/scottish-
cafe-and-restaurant. Mon–Wed & Fri–Sat
9am–5pm, Thurs 9am–7pm, Sun 10am–5pm.

Beneath the National Gallery
with gorgeous views east across
Princes Street Gardens and the Old
Town, Contini's unique position,
contemporary design and fine
Scottish cuisine makes it a popular
lunch time target for well-heeled
office workers. The £20 three-
course menu includes pigeon breast
with blueberry dressing and Cullen
Skink, or you can just stop in for
tea and cake.

Number One

MAP P.68, POCKET MAP C14

The Balmoral Hotel, 1 Princes St ☎ 0131
5576727, ⓦ roccofortehotels.com. Daily
6–10pm.

Edinburgh's most reputable and
expensive restaurant set within the

Balmoral Hotel complex. Opt for the £89 seven-course tasting menu and you can expect a cacophony of colours, foams and flavours to challenge your palate.

Taco Mazama

MAP P.68, POCKET MAP A14

95 Princes St ☎ 0131 225 4729, ⓦ taco mazama.co.uk. Mon–Thurs 8am–9pm, Fri 8am–10pm, Sat 11am–10pm, Sun 11am–7pm.

Small Scottish chain selling inauthentic but tasty Mexican street food. The tacos, fajitas and burritos start from a mere £5.

Twenty Princes Street

MAP P.68, POCKET MAP C13

First floor, 20 Princes St ☎ 0131 652 7370, ⓦ twentyprincesstreet.co.uk. Daily noon–10.30pm.

This ambitious fine dining restaurant could be the next big thing on Edinburgh's dining circuit. Specializing in charcoal grilled meat and game served with exciting accompaniments like smoked bone marrow with garlic and herb crumb. Mains start from £14.50.

Pubs

The Black Bull

MAP P.68, POCKET MAP D13

43 Leith St ☎ 0131 557 5121, ⓦ theblackbull-edinburgh.co.uk. Sun–Thurs 11am–1am, Fri–Sat 11am–2am.

A true veteran, this classic old rock pub has defied the gentrification processes that have, in recent years, swallowed up most of its contemporaries. Expect a good range of bourbons, a solid jukebox and a lively body of regulars.

Bunker

MAP P.68, POCKET MAP D13

2–6 Calton Rd ☎ 0131 557 2925, ⓦ pivo-edinburgh.co.uk. Daily 11pm–3am.

You might recognise this bar's exterior from the memorable opening sequence of the cult film, *Trainspotting*. The bar makes little

The Café Royal Circle Bar

mention of its famous cameo and instead promotes itself as a Czech beer cellar, live music and pre and post club hangout.

Café Royal Circle Bar

MAP P.68, POCKET MAP C13

17 West Register St ☎ 0131 556 1884, ⓦ caferoyaledinburgh.co.uk. Mon–Wed 11am–11pm, Thurs 11am–midnight, Fri–Sat 10am–1pm, Sun 11am–10pm.

Worth a visit just for its splendid Victorian decor, notably the huge elliptical island bar and tiled portraits of renowned inventors. Although the pub has a somewhat transient clientele as office workers and well-healed shoppers duck in and out for a quick half and an oyster or two, the atmosphere here is perfectly genial and conversations are refreshingly audible.

The Voodoo Rooms

MAP P.68, POCKET MAP C13

19a West Register St ☎ 0131 556 7060, ⓦ thevoodoorooms.com. Mon–Thurs 4pm–1am, Fri–Sun noon–1am.

Glamorous and stylish Victorian bar, dining room and events space that attracts a dressed-up crowd, especially at the weekend. Frequent live music, performance and club nights, including Edinburgh's legendary retro swing, jive and R n'B extravaganza, Vegas!

The New Town

The New Town, itself well over two hundred years old, stands in total contrast to the Old Town: the streets are broad and straight, and most of the buildings are Neoclassical. Originally intended to be residential, the entire area, right down to the names of its streets, is something of a celebration of the Union, which, at the time building began in 1767, was nevertheless far from universally popular. Today, the New Town's main streets form the bustling hub of the city's commercial, retail and business life, dominated by shops, banks and offices. In many ways, the layout of the greater New Town is its own most remarkable sight, an extraordinary grouping of squares, circuses, terraces, crescents and parks that display a restrained symmetry. On the ground, many buildings offer their own individual variances of the architectural theme, particularly on the key thoroughfares of Queen and George Street, and Charlotte and St Andrew Square.

George Street

Lined with designer outlets, boutique shops, cocktail bars and flashy restaurants, **George Street** is by far the most interesting and

Melville Monument in St Andrew Square

attractive thoroughfare in the New Town. Most of the original Neoclassical buildings here survive even though their intended purpose as residential housing has long since expired. One original that didn't make it was the old Physician's Hall, demolished early in Victoria's reign to make way for The Dome, a spectacular Greco-Roman building with an ostentatious interior testament to the wealth and power of the bank that made its headquarters there.

Three main thoroughfares cut perpendicularly across George Street – each with an important statue at the intersection; those of Church of Scotland leader, Thomas Chalmers, Prime Minister Pitt the Younger and King George III – and each offer a decent melange of independent and chain shops, cafés and restaurants.

St Andrew Square

MAP P.78, POCKET MAP C13

Lying at the eastern end of George Street is the smartly landscaped

A bedroom at The Georgian House

St Andrew Square, whose centre is marked by the Melville Monument, a towering column topped by a statue of Lord Melville, Pitt the Younger's Navy Treasurer. Around the edge of the square you'll find Edinburgh's bus station, the city's swankiest shopping arcade, Multrees Walk, and a handsome eighteenth-century town mansion, designed by Sir William Chambers. Still the ceremonial headquarters of the Royal Bank of Scotland, the palatial mid-nineteenth-century banking hall is a symbol of the success of the New Town.

Charlotte Square

MAP P.78, POCKET MAP C4

At the western end of George Street, Charlotte Square was designed by Robert Adam in 1791, a year before his death. For the most part, his plans were faithfully implemented, an exception being the domed and porticoed church of St George, simplified on grounds of expense. Generally regarded as the epitome of the New Town's elegant simplicity, the square was once the most exclusive residential address in Edinburgh, and though much of it is now occupied by offices, the imperious dignity of the architecture is still clear to see. Indeed, the north

side, the finest of Adam's designs, is once again the city's premier address, with the official residence of the First Minister of the Scottish Government at no. 6 (Bute House), the Edinburgh equivalent of 10 Downing Street.

The Georgian House

MAP P.78, POCKET MAP C4

7 Charlotte Sq ☎ 0131 225 2160, ⓦ nts.org. uk. March & Nov daily 11am–4pm, April–Oct daily 10am–5pm, early Dec Thurs–Sun 11am–4pm. Closed mid-Dec–Feb £7.50, NTS.
Restored by the National Trust for Scotland, the interior of this residential townhouse provides a revealing sense of well-to-do New Town living in the early nineteenth century. Though a little stuffy and lifeless, the rooms are impressively decked out in period **furniture** – look for the working barrel organ which plays a selection of Scottish airs – and hung with fine **paintings**, including portraits by Scottish artists Sir Henry Raeburn and Allan Ramsay, seventeenth-century Dutch cabinet pictures and the beautiful *Marriage of the Virgin* by El Greco's teacher, the Italian miniaturist Giulio Clovio. In the basement you can see the original wine cellar, lined with roughly made bins, and a **kitchen** complete with an open fire

for roasting and a separate oven for baking; video reconstructions of life below and above stairs are shown in a nearby room.

Queen Street

MAP P.78, POCKET MAP D4

The last of the New Town's three main streets and the least tarnished by post-Georgian development. **Queen Street**'s southern side is occupied mostly by offices, while across the road there's a huge private residents' garden. There are few individual attractions here, with the exception of the **Scottish National Portrait Gallery** at the eastern end, just to the north of St Andrew Square.

Scottish National Portrait Gallery

MAP P.78, POCKET MAP B13
1 Queen St ☎ 0131 624 6200,
ⓦ nationalgalleries.org. Fri–Wed 10am–5pm, Thurs 10am–7pm. Free.

Housed in a fantastic Gothic Revivalist palace in red sandstone, the **Scottish National Portrait Gallery** makes an extravagant contrast to the New Town's prevailing Neoclassicism. The exterior of the building is encrusted with statues of national heroes, a theme reiterated in the stunning two-storey entrance hall by William Hole's tapestry-like frieze and mural, carefully restored in the building's revamp.

The gallery's collection extends to over thirty thousand images with seventeen exhibition spaces exploring the differing characteristics of Scotland as a nation and a people. Inevitably oil paintings of the likes of Mary, Queen of Scots and Robert Burns form the backbone of the collection, but there's a lot to be said for the contemporary portraits that often show a country in cultural flux. One such recent exhibition showed

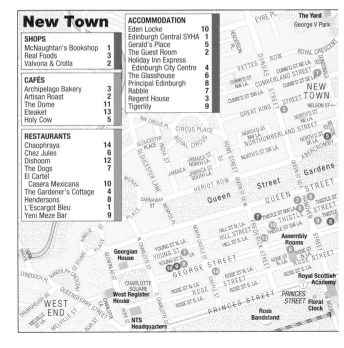

Edinburgh's Art Scene

With a backdrop as aesthetic as Edinburgh's, it's little wonder that the city's art scene thrives not only in the main galleries, but on the streets through market sales and in independent outlets.

If your visit to Edinburgh coincides with the end of the academic year then the huge Degree Show at the prestigious College of Art is well worth a good couple of hour's inspection. Just prior to this is the Hidden Door alternative arts festival (see page 144), a volunteer run bonanza of visual art instalments, music and various other creative outlets.

For more established artists' exhibitions, the best place to go is Dundas Street in the New Town where you'll find a cluster of reputable independent galleries within feet of one another.

EDINBURGH COLLEGE OF ART

74 Lauriston Place ☎ 0131 651 5800 ⊕ eca.ed.ac.uk. Degree show early June, masters degree show August. Free.

An increasingly popular event on the art calendar, the Degree Show attracts private collectors and gallery owners hoping to scout out the best of this year's crop of graduating students. The output on display is always diverse and on the whole – for better or worse – much bolder than you would find in a commercial gallery.

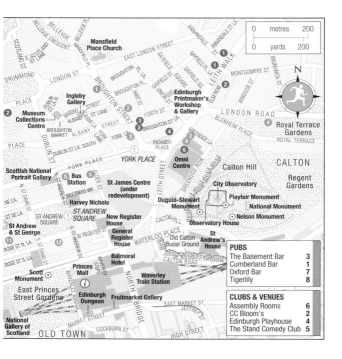

Scottish photographer, Graham MacIndoe's own harrowing descent into heroin addiction, a scourge that was at epidemic levels in the housing schemes of Leith in the late 80s.

Beyond the collection and exhibitions the gallery organises tours, art classes and even the occasional harp recital.

Broughton Street

MAP P.78, POCKET MAP E3

Over the years this short stretch of New Town tarmac has established itself a foodie hotspot with a combination of faddish bars and diners, traditional Victorian boozers and fine dining restaurants. It all stemmed from the opening of Real Foods, an organic supermarket in the mid-70s that drew in punters from across the city and beyond. More innovators have since moved in including Artisan Roast who were at the helm of the coffee revolution, personally sourcing and roasting their own beans before it was all the rage.

It's not just cafés and restaurants here however, boutique shops fill the gaps with artisan produce on sale from clothes to Scandinavian haberdashery.

Mansfield Place Church

MAP P.78, POCKET MAP E3

Mansfield Place ☏ 0131 474 8013, ⓦ mansfieldtraquair.org.uk. Viewing of the murals: Sept–July second Sun each month 1–4pm, Aug has more viewings, check website.

The highlight of the Broughton Street area is the neo-Norman **Mansfield Place Church**. It contains a cycle of murals by the Dublin-born Phoebe Anna Traquair, a leading light in the Scottish Arts and Crafts movement. Covering vast areas of the walls and ceilings of the main nave

The Gardens of the New Town

Designed to relieve the wanton overcrowding of Edinburgh's medieval Old Town that had left the city in the grip of the mid-seventeenth-century plague, James Craig's New Town design was deliberately spacious with wide boulevards, attractive squares and mansion houses with, revolutionarily, huge communal parkland. The pungent Nor' Loch that had for centuries absorbed the city's effluent was drained to produce Princes Street Gardens. To the North of the original New Town at Queen Street, a similar near symmetrical garden was created.

It was a popular idea and when further proposals to expand the New Town to the north, east and west from the 1800s were put together, gardens played a fundamental role in the designs. Many were small and fitted into residential crescents or squares; however, some were enormous and set in beautiful and dramatic scenery. The forested Dean Gardens just downstream from Dean Village (see page 87) on the Water of Leith, for example, has breathtaking views onto Dean Bridge, St Bernard's Well and a mighty waterfall. Regent Gardens, the largest private park in town occupies a huge tranche of Calton hill and has tennis courts, a putting green and a ha-ha.

Visiting the gardens can be problematic, because with the exception of Princes Street Gardens and St Andrew Square, most are privately owned by local residents. Occasional open days are announced and gardens sometimes open their gates during the Open Doors weekend (ⓦ doorsopendays.org.uk) in September.

Edinburgh Printmakers

and side chapels, the wonderfully luminous paintings depict biblical parables and texts, with rows of angels, cherubs flecked with gold and worshipping figures painted in delicate pastel colours.

Museum Collections Centre

MAP P.78, POCKET MAP E3
10 Broughton Market ☎ 0131 556 9536, Ⓦ edinburghmuseums.org.uk. First Tues of the month at 2pm or by appointment Wed–Sat 10am–5pm, Sun noon–5pm. Free.
One of a pair of warehouses in the city the Museum Collections Centre in Broughton Market (along with its sister depository in Granton) holds the reserve collections for Edinburgh's main museums. Uniquely and unbeknownst to the majority of locals, both open their doors to the public for guided tours. Naturally the experience is very different to a normal museum; artefacts are racked tightly together and there's no item descriptions or expensive café here, but you do get a sense of privilege being able to have a good nose around.

The collection is particularly focussed on Edinburgh's own heritage with artefacts through the centuries that either were made in the city or used there. More recent items like Chopper bikes or shop signs rub shoulders with the original model for the Scott Monument, cannonballs and even bags of archeological soil.

With around one hundred and thirty thousand items held here it's impossible to see it all, but if you have a particular area of interest you can book a free tailored tour.

Edinburgh Printmakers

MAP P.78, POCKET MAP F3
23 Union St ☎ 0131 557 2479, Ⓦ edinburghprintmakers.co.uk. Tues–Sat 10am–6pm. Free.
Established in the late 60s as the first open access studio in the country, the **Edinburgh Printmakers** workshop and gallery provides the opportunity for artists to engage in the practice of fine-art printmaking including etching, lithography and digital. Visitors can peer down at the artists at work from a balcony or even get involved themselves by signing up to one of the courses offered here. Exhibitions are always running too – which are free to enter – and there's also a decent shop where you can pick up prints and gifts on the way out.

Shops

McNaughtan's Bookshop

MAP P.78, POCKET MAP F3

3a–4a Haddington Place, Leith Walk
☎ 0131 556 5897, ⓦ mcnaughtans.co.uk.
Tues–Sat 11am–5pm.

Probably Edinburgh's oldest purveyor of antiquarian literature. Housed in a beautiful old basement, there's also a contemporary art exhibition space.

Real Foods

MAP P.78, POCKET MAP E3

37 Broughton St, New Town ☎ 0131 557 1911, ⓦ realfoods.co.uk; Mon–Fri 8am–9pm, Sat 9am–6.30pm, Sun 10am–6pm.

Edinburgh's long-standing supermarket for wholefoods, organic produce and niche products that can't be found elsewhere in town. The range here is vast, making it a must for those with special diets or an interest in discovering new and curious foods.

Valvona & Crolla

MAP P.78, POCKET MAP F3

19 Elm Row, Leith Walk ☎ 0131 556 6066, ⓦ valvonacrolla.co.uk. Mon–Thurs 8.30am–6pm, Fri & Sat 8am–6.30pm, Sun 10am–6pm.

McNaughtan's Bookshop

Edinburgh's oldest and most venerated deli, with Italian market produce personally imported weekly from Milan.

Cafés

Archipelago Bakery

MAP P.78, POCKET MAP D3

39 Dundas St, New Town ☎ 07932 462715, ⓦ archipelagobakery.co.uk. Mon–Sat 9am–5pm.

Serving up some of Edinburgh's crustiest loaves, you can sit and drink coffee here while marvelling at the mouth-watering breads, pies and pastries thrust out of the ovens in view.

Artisan Roast

MAP P.78, POCKET MAP E3

57 Broughton St ☎ 07522 321 893, ⓦ artisanroast.co.uk; Mon–Fri 8am–6.30pm, Sat–Sun 9am–6.30pm.

A seemingly unstoppable force in the connoisseur coffee roasters' market, *Artisan Roast*'s sweet, nutty brews are found in independent cafés all over town these days, but this narrow, grungy shop with hessian beans bags for decor and obligatorily bearded baristas is where their revolution started.

The Dome

MAP P.78, POCKET MAP B13

14 George St ☎ 0131 624 8624, ⓦ thedome edinburgh.com. Daily 10am–midnight

Ludicrously opulent, this early Victorian complex of cafés, restaurants and bars is a feast for the eyes. It's an unashamed melange of Corinthian columns, marbled floors and chandeliers topped off with a huge glass dome. Afternoon tea is £18.50 and two course menus cost £16.

Eteaket

MAP P.78, POCKET MAP A13

41a Frederick St ☎ 0131 226 2982, ⓦ eteaket.co.uk. Daily 9am–6pm.

The best of the tea boutiques in the city centre, with a restrained but contemporary decor scheme and tables outside. Order from their exotic range of loose teas like the award-winning silver needle (a white tea) and you'll be served a petite pot alongside a timer so you know exactly when to end the steeping process.

Holy Cow

MAP P.78, POCKET MAP E3
34 Elder St Ⓦ bit.ly/holycowed. Mon–Sat 10am–10pm, Sun 10am–6pm.
Bright, friendly vegan café next to the bus station that specialises in jackfruit burgers, egg free cakes and dairy free lattes. The menu is small and experimental, with bizarre but tasty creations like the "fish" burger – celeriac wrapped in seaweed – and chips for £10.50.

Restaurants

Chaophraya

MAP P.78, POCKET MAP D4
33 Castle St Ⓣ 0131 226 7614, Ⓦ chaophraya.co.uk. Mon–Sat noon–10.30pm, Sun noon–10pm.
Thai rooftop restaurant with a "Glassbox" section that has a near 360-degree view of the city. The menu is stunning too, and reasonably priced; if you go veggie, the set meal is just £25, while on the à la carte there are plenty interesting sea food choices like soft shell crab tempura for £12.50 and steamed bass in a chilli and lime sauce for £17.50.

Chez Jules

MAP P.78, POCKET MAP B13
109 Hanover St Ⓣ 0131 226 6992, Ⓦ chezjulesbistro.com. Mon–Thurs & Sun noon–11pm, Fri & Sat noon–midnight.
Run by the former boss of the once mighty Pierre Victoire bistro chain. The formula is much the same: cheap and generous set menus, good table wine and an informal setting. Your two-course lunch (£7.90) might include French onion soup and beef bourguignon with fries.

The Dogs

Dishoom

MAP P.78, POCKET MAP C13
3a St Andrew Square Ⓣ 0131 202 6406, Ⓦ dishoom.com. Mon–Wed 8am–11pm, Thurs–Sat 8am–noon, Sun 9am–11pm.
Recreating all the trappings of Old Bombay's Persian cafés; all that's missing is the sweat dripping off your chin. Diners receive a ridiculously effusive welcome followed by the patience-of-an-Indian-saint waiting staff as you endeavour to comprehend the extensive menu. Pick the Pau Bhaji for £4.50 – curry and a homemade roll – and the devilishly smoky gunpowder potatoes for £6.50 and you'll be off to a flying start.

The Dogs

MAP P.78, POCKET MAP A13
110 Hanover St Ⓣ 0131 220 1208, Ⓦ thedogsonline.co.uk. Mon–Fri noon–2.30pm & 6–10pm, Sat noon–4pm & 5–10pm, Sun noon–4pm & 6–10pm.
Scottish gastro-pub cooking taken to a whole new level with confident use of traditional ingredients paired with modern flavours such as the ox cheek burger, skirlie (oats and onions fried in lard) and barbeque sauce for £7.

L'Escargot Bleu

Over the past fifty years Hendersons has evolved from a veggie canteen into a gourmet institution and arts centre. At street level there's a deli and bakery with a vegan bistro around the corner, while the canteen below still bashes out a superb feast of salads and hot comfort food, buffet style, where you can fill up for around £10 to £13.

L'Escargot Bleu

MAP P.78, POCKET MAP E3
56 Broughton St ☎ 0131 557 1600,
🌐 lescargotbleu.co.uk. Mon–Thurs noon–2.30pm & 5.30–10pm, Fri & Sat noon–3pm & 5.30–10.30pm.
A big step on from the rustic, no-frills French bistro of yesteryear, here classic French country cooking is brought to bear on a range of locally sourced produce, as in the Barra snails or the Orkney beef. Two-course lunch and pre-theatre menus are a snip at £13 and £15 respectively.

Yeni Meze Bar

MAP P.78, POCKET MAP B13
73 Hanover St ☎ 0131 225 5755,
🌐 yenirestaurant.com Mon–Thurs noon–9pm, Fri–Sat noon–10pm.
Specializing in lamb kofte and *imam bayildi* (baked aubergine dish), this is ultimately a Turkish restaurant that draws in additional dishes from around the Med, like their Italian arancini. Go for the £16 banquet and see the delights that keep arriving.

El Cartel Casera Mexicana

MAP P.78, POCKET MAP A13
64 Thistle St ☎ 0131 226 7171,
🌐 elcartelmexicana.co.uk. Mon–Thurs & Sun noon–10pm, Sat noon–midnight.
Mexican *antojitos* (tapas-sized street food from £4–10) served with funky margaritas in a cool setting that draws heavily from the Día de los Muertos festival. Tacos, street corn and quesadillas feature on the menu as well as oddities like shredded ox patties.

The Gardener's Cottage

MAP P.78, POCKET MAP F3
1 Royal Terrace Gardens, London Rd
☎ 0131 558 1221, 🌐 thegardenerscottage. co. Wed–Mon noon–2.30pm & 5–10pm.
In an achingly beautiful little cottage, uniquely sited in a parkland setting. Dining is intimate, in two small rooms with communal long tables, while the open kitchen is stamp-sized. Save for dietary requirement adjustments, there's no choice here, just seven outstanding courses of Scottish design for £50.

Hendersons

MAP P.78, POCKET MAP A13
94 Hanover St ☎ 0131 225 2131,
🌐 hendersonsofedinburgh.co.uk. Mon–Thurs 8am–9pm, Fri–Sat 8am–10pm, Sun 10.30–4pm.

Pubs

The Basement Bar

MAP P.78, POCKET MAP E3
10a–12a Broughton St ☎ 0131 557 0097,
🌐 basement-bar-edinburgh.co.uk. Daily 11am–1am. Food served 11am–8pm.
Mexican cantina and cocktail bar that celebrates everything about Mexico that's cool, from the Día de muertos decor to the reputable kitchen that has been churning out top notch burritos and enchiladas for over two decades.

For something a little different, the smoky jackfruit chilli for £11 has a mighty kick, especially when augmented with the accompanying bottle of house chipotle.

Cumberland Bar

MAP P.78, POCKET MAP D3

1–3 Cumberland St ☎ 0131 558 3134, ⓦ cumberlandbar.co.uk. Mon–Wed noon–midnight, Thurs–Sat noon–1am, Sun 11am–midnight.

This lovely old pub is just far enough off the beaten track to remain free from the weekend's pub-crawling masses. Its other great assets are its willow-shaded beer garden and fantastic assortment of cask ales.

Oxford Bar

MAP P.78, POCKET MAP C4

8 Young St ☎ 0131 539 7119, ⓦ oxfordbar. co.uk. Mon–Thurs noon–midnight, Fri & Sat 11am–1am, Sun 12.30–11pm.

Unpretentious, unspoilt, no-nonsense city bar – which is why local crime writer Ian Rankin and his Inspector Rebus like it so much. Fans duly make the pilgrimage, but fortunately not all the regulars have been scared off.

Tigerlily

MAP P.78, POCKET MAP C4

125 George St ☎ 0131 225 5005, ⓦ tigerlily edinburgh.co.uk. Daily 7am–1am.

The daddy of all George Street's decadent destination bars, where the locals come to see and be seen. Partitioned into various lounges, each with their own boutique personality, there's room for intimacy here alongside the hen parties and cocktail-fuelled dance-floor posturing.

Clubs and venues

Assembly Rooms

MAP P.78, POCKET MAP A14

54 George St, New Town ☎ 0131 220 4348, ⓦ assemblyroomsedinburgh.co.uk.

This complex of small and large halls is used all year, but really comes into its own during the Fringe, featuring large-scale drama productions and mainstream comedy.

CC Bloom's

MAP P.78, POCKET MAP F3

23–24 Greenside Place, New Town ☎ 0131 556 9331. Daily 11am–3am.

Edinburgh's most enduring gay bar, with a big dancefloor, stonking rhythms, a young, friendly crowd and free entry all night.

Edinburgh Playhouse

MAP P.78, POCKET MAP F3

18–22 Greenside Place ☎ 0131 524 3333, ⓦ playhousetheatre.com.

The largest theatre in Britain with a capacity of over three thousand, the Playhouse is used largely for extended runs of popular musicals and occasional music concerts.

The Stand Comedy Club

MAP P.78, POCKET MAP E3

5 York Place, New Town ☎ 0131 558 7272, ⓦ thestand.co.uk.

The city's undisputed top comedy spot, with different acts on every night and some of the UK's top comics headlining at the weekends. Be sure to arrive early to secure a good table for the evening. Entry ranges wildly from £3 to £17.50.

Assembly Rooms

West End and Dean Village

Much of Edinburgh's wealth is concentrated in its West End, where embassies and lawyers occupy many of the huge Georgian townhouses west of Charlotte Square. On the main thoroughfares and in the pretty cobbled lanes of West End Village, attractive pubs, cafés and restaurants thrive on the affluent footfall from locals and office workers. Further prosperity can be found nearby; Edinburgh's theatre and financial districts that occupy the area south of Princes Street's western tip have seen major developments in recent times and gentrification has followed suit. On the West End's northern fringe the gradient drops sharply towards the Water of Leith, where the old milling settlement of Dean Village is an unexpected delight and a good place to begin exploring the city's less touristic treasures.

St Mary's Cathedral

MAP P.88, POCKET MAP B5
Palmerston Place ☎ 0131 225 6293,
ⓦ cathedral.net. Daily 8am–7.30pm;
Evensong Mon–Sat 5.30pm. Sun 3.30pm.
Free (some guest performances charge).

With its trio of soaring spires **St Mary's Cathedral** stabs deep into the city's western horizon. On closer inspection the cathedral is no less

St Mary's Cathedral

impressive. Entered through its ornamental Gothic portal, your eye is immediately drawn ahead to the stained-glass window triplet above the raised altar. The high vault, supported by a run of symmetrical Gothic arches give the place uniquely rich acoustics as can be witnessed most days during Evensong, sung by the Cathedral Choir. Lunchtime chamber concerts are also a regular feature here as are guest choirs and organist performances.

West End Village

MAP P.88, POCKET MAP B5

The name "**West End Village**" is a recent concoction coined to market the unspoiled Georgian shopping lanes of William Street. A popular filming location thanks to its cobbles, Victorian street lamps and shop frontages – with their original cast iron balconies – it's a charming area for a short stroll and a cappuccino away from the hustle of the city centre. There are also some nice pubs, one (*The Melville*) with tables outside where you can sink a cold one while watching the city's elite swan in and out of the

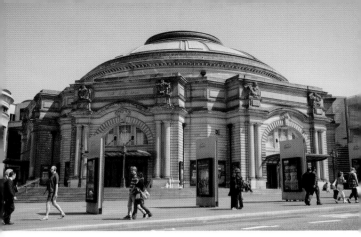

Usher Hall in Edinburgh's Theatre District

street's numerous boutique shops and beauty salons.

Edinburgh Gin

MAP P.88, POCKET MAP C5

1a Rutland Square ☎ 0131 656 2810, ⓦ edinburghgin.com. Daily 10am–5pm. Tours £10–£25.

Right in step with current drinking trends, **Edinburgh Gin** is a small independent distiller that takes pride in the city's three-hundred-year gin production heritage. A number of tours are offered where you can see the beautiful copper stills in action, learn about the production techniques and recipes and perhaps experience a tutored tasting session.

Theatre District

MAP P.88, POCKET MAP C5

With some of the city's more highbrow theatres rubbing shoulders with its less salubrious late bars, Edinburgh's Theatre District, located on and around Lothian Road, has always had a somewhat Jekyll and Hyde reputation. But these days more than a whiff of gentrification hangs in the air. Modern bars and contemporary kitchens – as they like to be known – are opening in every nip and tuck, competing with the old Italian stalwarts that have been knocking out pizzas late into the

night for generations. The draw, of course, are the theatres themselves, and most attractive of the bunch is the Edwardian Usher Hall. Sandwiched between the Georgian Lyceum and the tiny Traverse theatres, it was built in the classical style barely seen since Queen Vic was a child and similar in shape, if not size, to London's Royal Albert Hall. A little further south, look out for the vast complex housing the Odeon cinema, one of only a handful of Art Deco buildings in town.

Edinburgh Farmers' Market

MAP P.88, POCKET MAP D5

Castle Terrace ⓦ edinburghfarmersmarket. co.uk. Sat 9am–2pm.

Round the back of the Usher Hall, the wide pavements of Castle Terrace with its towering backdrop of the castle provide a convivial setting for the **Edinburgh Farmers' Market**. Unlike the city's other producer's markets, the focus here is more on groceries than street food although you can still get a coffee and a cake and, if you're lucky, a seat.

Dean Village

Less than half a mile from Princes Street's western end, the old milling community of **Dean Village** is one of central Edinburgh's most

The Water of Leith in Dean Village

up on both sides, the ancient settlement dating back at least as far as the twelfth century has a self-contained air. Developed in isolation, the village's warren of lanes and footpaths weave through a unique assortment of architectural styles, from rubble-stone cottages and mews houses to the ambitious Well Court; a colossal social housing complex that closely resembles a Victorian mansion. The village is bookended by beautiful waterfalls and glorious walks can be enjoyed in either direction along the Water of Leith.

Dean Bridge

MAP P.88, POCKET MAP B4

High above Dean Village, **Dean Bridge**, a bravura feat of 1830s engineering by Thomas Telford, carries the main road over 100ft above the river. It marks one of the world's first village bypasses, meaning townsfolk and traders no

picturesque yet unexpected corners, its atmosphere of decay arrested by the conversion of numerous granaries and tall mill buildings into designer flats. Nestling close to the river, with steep banks rising

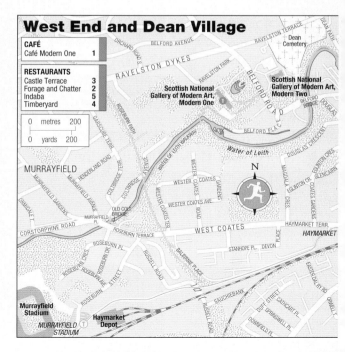

West End and Dean Village

CAFÉ	
Café Modern One	1

RESTAURANTS	
Castle Terrace	3
Forage and Chatter	2
Indaba	5
Timberyard	4

longer needed to enter Dean village when travelling between Edinburgh and Queensferry. Consequently, its construction marked a steep decline in the prosperity of the village, only arrested in recent decades as the settlement's mills were converted into residential housing.

Scottish National Gallery of Modern Art

MAP P.88, POCKET MAP A5

75 Belford Rd ☏ 0131 624 6200, ⊛ national galleries.org. Daily 10am–5pm (till 6pm in Aug). Free; entrance charge for some temporary exhibitions. A free bus service connects the National Gallery of Scotland with the Modern One and Two galleries (outbound: daily 11am–4pm, every hour on the hour except 1pm; return: 11.30am, 12.30pm, 2.30pm, 3.30pm & 5pm).

The first collection in Britain devoted solely to post-1800s painting and sculpture is housed across two distinctive Neoclassical buildings, **Modern One** and **Modern Two**. Its grounds serve as a **sculpture park**, featuring works by, among others, Charles Jencks, whose prize-winning *Landform*, a swirling mix of ponds and grassy mounds, dominates the area in front of Modern One.

The art collection here has a strong Scottish contingent, with a particularly fine body of works from the early twentieth-century **Colourists**. The collection's **international paintings** feature crowd-pleasing names like Matisse and Picasso, while Hockney, Warhol and Freud form the backbone of a solid post-war catalogue.

The work of Edinburgh-born sculptor **Sir Eduardo Paolozzi**, described by some as the father of Pop Art, features comprehensively in Modern Two. To the right of the main entrance, his London studio has been expertly re-created, right down to the clutter of half-finished casts, toys and empty pots of glue.

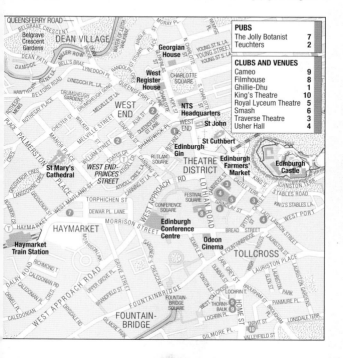

PUBS

| The Jolly Botanist | 7 |
| Teuchters | 2 |

CLUBS AND VENUES

Cameo	9
Filmhouse	8
Ghillie-Dhu	1
King's Theatre	10
Royal Lyceum Theatre	5
Smash	6
Traverse Theatre	3
Usher Hall	4

Café

Café Modern One

MAP P.88, POCKET MAP A5
Scottish National Gallery of Modern
Art, 75 Belford Rd ☎ 0131 332 8600,
Ⓦ heritageportfolio.co.uk. Mon–Fri
9am–4.30pm, Sat & Sun 10am–4.30pm.
One of the nicest cafés in
Edinburgh thanks to its delightful
walled garden round the back
of the Modern One gallery. The
canteen here serves up superb
healthy lunches including a range
of vibrant homemade salads; three
per person should suffice for £6.

Restaurants

Castle Terrace

MAP P.88, POCKET MAP D5
33–35 Castle Terrace ☎ 0131 229 1222,
Ⓦ castleterracerestaurant.com. Tues–Sat
noon–2pm & 6–10pm.
Arguably Edinburgh's best fine-
dining restaurant bringing high-level
French cooking to bear on quality
Scottish produce. Head straight for
the £80 tasting menu, otherwise try
the three-course lunch at £33.

Castle Terrace

Forage and Chatter

MAP P.88, POCKET MAP C5
1A Alva St ☎ 0131 225 4599,
Ⓦ forageandchatter.com. Tues–Sat
noon–2.30pm & 6–11pm.
Showcasing the best of Scotland's
produce sourced within a 25-mile
radius, this concept restaurant
garners more accolades these
days than any other in town. The
distance limitation doesn't seem
to affect the offerings here, which
regularly include the ruminants in
the city limit hill farms as well as a
range of North Sea fish. Mains are
around £17.

Indaba

MAP P.88, POCKET MAP C6
3 Lochrin Terrace ☎ 0131 221 1554,
Ⓦ edindaba.co.uk; Mon–Thurs 5–9.30pm,
Fri & Sat 5–10pm.
An unlikely combination of South
African and northern Spanish
cuisine, this modest restaurant
delivers some interesting tapas.
The African contributions are
predominantly meaty, like the
boerewors sausage with chakalaka
for £8, while the Spanish plates are
typically vibrant and colourful.

Timberyard

MAP P.88, POCKET MAP A16
10 Cambridge St ☎ 0131 221 1222,
Ⓦ timberyard.co. Tues–Sat noon–2pm &
5.30–9.30pm.
This swanky yet somehow rustic
old workshop makes for a genial
atmosphere with its shared,
candlelit indoor benches and
sunny courtyard garden. The
food focuses on high-quality
Scottish produce, where unfamiliar
bedfellows like mackerel,
nasturtium and buttermilk come
together on one plate as part of a
four-course £55 menu.

Pubs

The Jolly Botanist

MAP P.88, POCKET MAP B5
256–260 Morrison St ☎ 0131 228 5596,

Ⓦ thejollybotanist.co.uk. Sun–Thurs 10am–midnight, Fri & Sat 10am–1am.
Riding on the back of gin drinking's phenomenal comeback, this new bar has made a name for itself for its range of eclectic liquor sourced from micro-distilleries around the globe.

Teuchters

MAP P.88, POCKET MAP B5
26 William St Ⓣ 0131 225 2973,
Ⓦ teuchtersbar.co.uk. Mon–Sat 10.30am–1am; food 10.30am–10pm.
The more traditional of the three-pub cluster in William Street and at times the most lively. It's a free house with a good range of Scottish cask ales and a menu of honest Scottish pub grub like haggis stovies for £8.25.

Clubs and venues

Cameo

MAP P.88, POCKET MAP C6
38 Home St, Tollcross Ⓣ 0871 902 5723,
Ⓦ picturehouses.com.
A treasure of an arthouse cinema with a cosy wee bar – opened by Sean Connery – attached; screens more challenging mainstream releases and cult late-nighters.

Filmhouse

MAP P.88, POCKET MAP C5
88 Lothian Rd Ⓣ 0131 228 2688,
Ⓦ filmhousecinema.com.
Three-screen cinema and home to the city's international film festival that shows an eclectic programme of independent, art-house and classic films.

Ghillie-Dhu

MAP P.88, POCKET MAP C5
2 Rutland Place Ⓣ 0131 222 9930,
Ⓦ ghillie-dhu.co.uk. Mon–Fri 11am–3am, Sat & Sun 10am–3am. Ceilidh from 7pm.
Housed in a rather fancy auditorium, Ghillie-Dhu wholeheartedly embraces Scotland's traditional musical heritage. A rotation of accomplished folk groups plays throughout the week (free entry),

culminating in Friday and Saturday's jovial ceilidh nights (£7 entry).

King's Theatre

MAP P.88, POCKET MAP D6
2 Leven St Ⓣ 0131 529 6000,
Ⓦ edtheatres.com/kings.
Edwardian civic theatre majoring in pantomime, touring West End plays and the occasional drama or opera performance. The interior is surprisingly luxurious, with marble staircases, carved mahogany doors and a sumptuously regal auditorium.

Royal Lyceum Theatre

MAP P.88, POCKET MAP C5
30 Grindlay St Ⓣ 0131 248 4848,
Ⓦ lyceum.org.uk.
A fine Victorian civic theatre and leading venue for mainstream drama. The theatre commissions around seven plays annually as well as hosting travelling productions.

Smash

MAP P.88, POCKET MAP C5
40–42 Grindlay St Ⓣ 0131 622 7086,
Ⓦ smash.me.uk. Open 7pm–3am on concert nights.
Small live music venue with a penchant for punk and new wave bands. Turns into a club after performances.

Traverse Theatre

MAP P.88, POCKET MAP C5
10 Cambridge St Ⓣ 0131 228 1404,
Ⓦ traverse.co.uk.
One of Britain's premier venues for new plays and avant-garde drama from around the world. Also has a lively and popular bar.

Usher Hall

MAP P.88, POCKET MAP C5
Lothian Rd Ⓣ 0131 228 1155,
Ⓦ usherhall.co.uk.
Reopened after a major refurbishment with a strikingly contemporary extension, Edinburgh's main civic concert hall frequently features choral and symphony concerts, as well as legends of country, jazz, world and pop.

Stockbridge

Between the New Town and the Botanic Gardens, the busy suburb of Stockbridge grew up around the Water of Leith ford (and its seventeenth-century bridge) over which cattle were driven to market in Edinburgh. The hamlet was essentially gobbled up in the expansion of the New Town, but a few charming buildings and an independent character prevail in the district today. The area is a popular quarter for young professionals who can't afford the property prices in the New Town proper, and as a result there's a good crop of bars, boutiques and places to eat along both Raeburn Place, the main road, and St Stephen Street, one of Edinburgh's more maverick side streets.

St Stephen Street

MAP P.94, POCKET MAP C3

Hosting some of the capital's more eccentric retailers perched above alluring basement restaurants and bars, **St Stephen Street** showcases the fashionable Stockbridge area's more bohemian side. Art lovers can peruse petite galleries, while yesteryear is celebrated in antique shops, a vinyl record seller and a couple of vintage fashion emporiums. The street's prosperity may be clear for all to see, but many residents can remember when this swanky corner of Georgian Edinburgh was but a slum. How times have changed.

Stockbridge Market

MAP P.94, POCKET MAP C3

Kerr St Ⓦ stockbridgemarket.com. Sun 10am–5pm.

Food stalls at Stockbridge Market

Water of Leith

MAP P.94, POCKET MAP B4

Slicing a diagonal cleft from the Pentland hills south west of town, the Water of Leith twists and churns its peaty, golden-brown burden towards the Shore, Leith's (and now Edinburgh's) attractive old harbour. En-route, although comfortably bypassing the city's Old Town, the river trundles by old villages that once depended on its power to drive mills. Nature abounds on this eminently walkable route towards the sea; swans and mallards are commonly seen under the canapé while otters, mink, dippers and kingfishers make sporadic appearances. Look out for the satellite attractions of the Modern Art Gallery (see page 89) at Dean Village, and the Royal Botanic Gardens (see page 94) near Stockbridge make another good draw from the river's edge. Downstream, the river's final twist opens wide at the Shore (see page 99) as the restaurants of the city's gourmet heart swim into view.

A consistently popular street-food destination, **Stockbridge Market** offers a bounty of artisan produce to eat on the hoof or take away. It's a compact affair, sited under a grove of leaning Sorbus trees by the banks of the Water of Leith, where the tightly packed stallholders supply a veritable feast for the senses. Even with the belligerent Scottish climate, there's somehow an international buzz as scores of locals and tourists dine out on paella or Bombay street food, or wash a cupcake down with a coffee served out of the back of a VW campervan.

The Yard

MAP P.94, POCKET MAP D2

22 Eyre Place Lane ☏ 0131 476 4506, ⓦ theyardscotland.org.uk. Sun 10am–5pm. Children £6 for 2 hrs, adults free.

One for the kids, **The Yard** is an exciting, bespoke adventure playground and activity centre designed by the BBC's *DIY SOS* programme. Geared towards children under 11, the focus here is on play how it used to be, with rope swings, roller skates, go-carts, chopper bikes and plenty of hiding places, while indoors there's an art room, books, instruments and a help-yourself café. A welcome and pleasingly anarchic antidote to the sterile, soft play proliferation of recent years.

Fettes College

MAP P.94, POCKET MAP A2

Regularly described as the "Eton of the North", and just like its southern rival, **Fettes College** proved it could also churn out prime ministerial material. Perhaps understandably, the school takes no credit for Tony Blair's achievements; one former teacher quipped that he was "the most difficult boy I ever had to deal with".

Another famous ex-pupil, in a fictional sense at least, was James Bond. Fleming had the agent board there for his teens as part of the *You Only Live Twice* back-story. Even Harry Potter can lay a claim to the school which, together with another of Edinburgh's private institutions (George Heriot's), inspired the concept of Hogwarts. Looking at the building it's not difficult to see why; its dramatic and unique hybridisation of French chateaux and the Scots Baronial style is an awe-inspiring sight, particularly when viewed from afar with its central tower thrusting out of the surrounding canopy.

the magnificent backdrop of old Edinburgh at arm's length.

Originally laid out in 1889, much of the grounds are set aside for rugby pitches intersected by a grid of tree-lined walk-ways, while at the eastern fringe, free tennis and basketball/football courts are lined up next to a petanque club and playground. There are also some attractive hidden corners to walk through. The lower part for instance has a large boating pond, home to many wildfowl thanks to the reed marsh at one end. Across the path is the sundial garden, a delightful, enclosed space with the centerpiece stone sundial from 1890 still standing.

Inverleith Park

Inverleith Park

MAP P.94, POCKET MAP B2

One of Scotland's largest urban gardens, **Inverleith Park** is a good place for a gentle stroll with

The Royal Botanic Garden

MAP P.94, POCKET MAP C2

Arboretum Place ☎ 0131 248 2909, 🌐 rbge.org.uk. Daily: March–Sept 10am–6pm; Feb & Oct 10am–5pm; Nov–Jan 10am–4pm (note that glasshouses close 1hr before garden). Garden free;

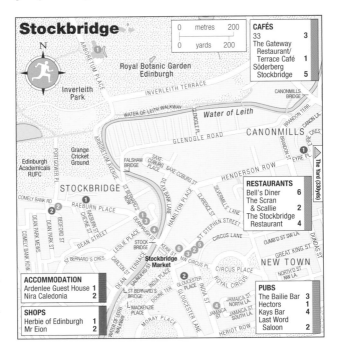

Stockbridge

| | metres | 200 |
| 0 | yards | 200 |

CAFÉS

33	3
The Gateway Restaurant/ Terrace Café	1
Söderberg Stockbridge	5

RESTAURANTS

Bell's Diner	6
The Scran & Scallie	2
The Stockbridge Restaurant	4

ACCOMMODATION

| Ardenlee Guest House | 1 |
| Nira Caledonia | 2 |

SHOPS

| Herbie of Edinburgh | 1 |
| Mr Eion | 2 |

PUBS

The Bailie Bar	3
Hectors	1
Kays Bar	4
Last Word Saloon	2

glasshouses £6.50; guided tours £6, tours last 1hr and leave from the John Hope Gateway at 11am and 2pm April–Oct. Just beyond the northern boundaries of the New Town is the seventy-acre site of the **Royal Botanic Garden**. Filled with mature trees and a huge variety of native and exotic plants and flowers, the "Botanics" (as they're commonly called) are most popular simply as a place to stroll and lounge around on the grass. The main entrance is the West Gate on Arboretum Place, through the contemporary, eco-designed John Hope Gateway, where you'll find interpretation areas, information, exhibitions, a shop and restaurant.

The northeastern fringe of the gardens has a series of ten glasshouses including a soaring 1850s Palm House, showing off a steamy array of palms, ferns, orchids, cycads and aquatic plants, including some huge circular water lilies. Pride of the collection here in recent years has been the titan arum plant which around June produces the world's largest flower. A notoriously stubborn plant to bloom, Edinburgh's specimen has been named Auld Reekie (Edinburgh's nickname) thanks to its fly attracting rotting flesh scent.

Outside, gardens of different themes are highlighted: the large Chinese-style garden, for example, has a bubbling waterfall and the world's largest collection of Asian wild plants outside China, while in the northwest corner there's a Scottish native woodland which effectively evokes the wild unkemptness of parts of the Scottish Highlands and west coast.

Art is also a strong theme within the Botanics, with a gallery showing changing contemporary exhibitions in the attractive eighteenth-century Inverleith House at the centre of the gardens. Scattered all around are a number of outdoor sculptures, including a giant pine cone by landscape artist Andy Goldsworthy and the striking stainless-steel east gate, designed in the form of stylized rhododendrons. Parts of the garden are also notable for their great vistas: the lawns near Inverleith House offer one of the city's best views of the Castle and Old Town's steeples and monuments.

The Victorian Palm House at The Royal Botanic Garden

Shops

Herbie of Edinburgh

MAP P.94, POCKET MAP B3
66 Raeburn Place ☎ 0131 332 9888,
🌐 herbieofedinburgh.co.uk. Mon–Fri
9am–7pm, Sat 9am–6pm.
Thriving little delicatessen packed
from top to toe with everything
from gourmet ingredients like wild
mushrooms, pickles and pastas to
ready-to-eat pies, tortillas and cakes.

Mr Eion

MAP P.94, POCKET MAP B3
9 Dean Park St ☎ 0131 343 1354,
🌐 mreion.com Wed, Fri & Sat 10am–5pm,
Thurs 10am–6pm, Sun 11am–3pm.
One for serious coffee drinkers, Mr
Eion is a small-batch bean roaster
selling bags out of their little lab off
Stockbridge's main drag. There's a
wide selection of single estate beans
on sale from around the globe with
accompanying tasting notes.

Cafés

33

MAP P.94, POCKET MAP C3
33 Deanhaugh St ☎ 0131 332 8353. Mon–Fri
8am–5pm, Sat 9am–6pm, Sun 10am–5pm.

Herbie of Edinburgh

Coffee and *pastel de natas* make
wonderful bedfellows, and this
busy – if a little cramped – café
sells the best custard tarts in town
alongside other tasty cakes and
sandwiches.

The Gateway Restaurant/
Terrace Café

MAP P.94, POCKET MAP C2
Royal Botanic Garden, Arboretum Place
☎ 0131 552 2674, 🌐 gatewayrestaurant.
net. Daily: March–Sept 10am–6pm; Feb &
Oct 10am–5pm; Nov–Jan 10am–4pm.
At the West Gate of the Botanics,
the John Hope Gateway Centre
has tables and a terrace overlooking
the gardens on its upper floor,
serving cream tea for £5 as well as
full breakfasts and posh lunches for
around £9 with many ingredients
grown in the gardens. A few hundred
yards beyond, the busy Terrace Café
serves coffees, snacks and less formal
lunches, with lots of outdoor tables
and kid-friendly options.

Söderberg

MAP P.94, POCKET MAP C3
3 Deanhaugh St ☎ 0131 332 2901,
🌐 soderberg.uk. Mon–Fri 8am–6pm, Sat &
Sun 9am–7pm.
Another side to the continental
baking scene, this time a Swedish
sourdough outfit with some
of the finest chewy, crusty
loaves in town. It's also a café
selling delicate cardamom
pastries (£2.50) to go with their
satisfyingly nutty coffees.

Restaurants

Bell's Diner

MAP P.94, POCKET MAP C3
7 St Stephen St ☎ 0131 225 8116,
🌐 bellsdineredinburgh.com. Sun & Mon
5–9pm, Tues–Fri 5–10pm, Sat 12.30–10pm.
Superb, veteran steak and burger
joint that's been knocking out
no-nonsense, homemade food since
the 70s. The menu is great value
with beef, chicken, lamb and nut
burgers ranging from £8 to £11.

The Scran & Scallie

MAP P.94, POCKET MAP B3
1 Comely Bank Rd ☎ 0131 332 6281,
ⓦ scranandscallie.com. Mon–Fri
noon–10pm, Sat & Sun 8.30am–10pm.
With its sister restaurants (Kitchin
and Castle Terrace) vying for
fine dining superiority, Scran &
Scallie sees celebrity chef, Tom
Kitchin taking on the gastropub
market. The food is truly top notch
if a little pricey, with mains –
including fish pie and homemade
sausage n' mash – ranging between
£13 and £19.

The Stockbridge Restaurant

MAP P.94, POCKET MAP C3
54 St Stephen St ☎ 0131 226 6766,
ⓦ thestockbridgerestaurant.co.uk. Tues–
Sat 7–9.30pm, Sun 7–9pm.
Basement restaurant with fine
linen, silverware and fancy platters
set alongside blackened stone walls
and a candlelit hearth. Save for
one veggie option, goat cheese,
aubergine and walnut frangipane,
it's meat, game and fish all the way,
but the quality is exceptional; the
two course set menu costs £28.

Pubs

The Bailie Bar

MAP P.94, POCKET MAP C3
2–4 St Stephen St. ☎ 0131 225 4673,
ⓦ thebailiebar.co.uk.
Mon–Thurs 11am–midnight, Fri & Sat
11am–1am, Sun 12.30pm–midnight.
Frothy cask ales in unpretentious
and often rowdy surroundings,
the Bailie's a traditional pub that's
been around long enough to
remember when this swanky corner
of Georgian Edinburgh was but
a slum.

Hectors

MAP P.94, POCKET MAP C3
47–49 Deanhaugh St ☎ 0131 343 1735,
ⓦ hectorsstockbridge.co.uk. Mon–Thurs
noon–midnight, Fri noon–1am, Sat
10am–1am, Sun 10am–midnight.

Kays Bar

The number one drinking
spot in Stockbridge for young
professionals, Hector's is a spacious
but intimate bar with good wines,
craft IPA and a creative bar menu
with mains like pepper and quinoa
burger with marmalade roast beets
for just shy of a tenner.

Kays Bar

MAP P.94, POCKET MAP C4
39 Jamaica St ☎ 0131 225 1858, ⓦ kaysbar.
co.uk. Mon–Thurs 11am–midnight, Fri & Sat
11am–1pm, Sun 12.30pm–11pm.
Tucked away in a New Town
side street, this former Georgian
coaching house was remodelled in
the Victorian era as a wine and spirit
merchant. Thankfully it has retained
its Victorian charm and now
operates as a cosy little pub serving
real ale and plenty of whiskies.

Last Word Saloon

MAP P.94, POCKET MAP C3
44 St Stephen St ☎ 0131 225 9009,
ⓦ lastwordsaloon.com. Daily 4pm–1am
Shadowy candlelit bar with open
fires and table service, where
an abundance of imaginative
homemade cocktails form the
backbone of the drinks menu.

Leith

Uber trendy Leith, Edinburgh's beating hipster heart, is a hub of creativity with its own distinct arts and music culture and cutting-edge dining scene. It has developed independently of the city up the hill, its history bound up in the hard graft of fishing, shipbuilding and trade. The presence of sailors and merchants has also historically given the place a cosmopolitan – if slightly rough – edge, still obvious today. Leith's initial revival from down-and-out port to des-res waterfront began in the 1980s around The Shore, the old harbour at the mouth of the Water of Leith. In recent years, the massive dock areas beyond have been transformed at a rate of knots, with landmark developments including Ocean Terminal, a shopping and entertainment complex, beside which the Royal Yacht Britannia has settled into her retirement.

Leith Links

MAP P.100, POCKET MAP C12

As its name would suggest, **Leith Links** has a historical golfing affiliation, in fact it was here that the first official rules that led to the modern game were developed in 1744. The sport was banned a few years after the links were formalised as a park in 1888 and today it's an attractive forty-six acre public space with tennis courts, bowling greens, a cricket club and community allotments. The perimeter and pathways, interestingly, host one of the largest collections of

Aerial view of Leith Links

The Banana Flats

Just a couple of blocks away from Leith's picturesque old harbour, Cables Wynd House (aka the **Banana Flats**) is arguably one of the most depressing examples of early 1960s **Brutalist** architecture in the country. Built to relieve overcrowding in the nearby tenements, the ten-storey wall of curved (hence its nickname) concrete and prison barred balconies is an unforgiving vision of apocalyptic decay.

Its low point came during the 80s when the flats became a focal point for Edinburgh's heroin epidemic, although things had calmed down by the time the building was used as a location in the hit film *Trainspotting*.

Talk of demolishing the flats was on the cards for years until a controversial 2017 decision to award the building **grade A listed status** – the same protection given to **Edinburgh Castle**.

mature elm trees in the country that are yet to succumb to Dutch Elm disease, while the lawns they surround are completely flat except for two unexpected hillocks. These are actually two of the remaining artillery mounds from the 1560 Siege of Leith – a standoff between the French and English armies.

Trinity House

MAP P.100, POCKET MAP B12
99 Kirkgate ☎ 0131 554 3289. Mon–Fri by appointment only. Free; HES.
Small appointment-only nautical museum housed in an attractive former guild hall, Trinity House possesses a decent collection of navigational paraphernalia, model ships and paintings. Photos also give a glimpse into Leith's old quayside prior to its decommissioning and subsequent regeneration.

The Shore

MAP P.100, POCKET MAP B11
The best way to absorb Leith's history and seafaring connections is to take a stroll along **The Shore**, a tenement-lined road running alongside the Water of Leith. Until the mid-nineteenth century this was a bustling and cosmopolitan **harbour**, visited by ships from all over the world, but as vessels

became increasingly large, they moored up at custom-built docks built beyond the original quays; these days, only a handful of boats are permanently moored here. Instead, the focus is on the numerous **pubs and restaurants** that line the street, many of which spill tables and chairs out onto the cobbled pavement on sunny days. And the dining here is good; within a few hundred yards of each other Leith has two Michelin-starred restaurants in *The Kitchin* and *Martin Wishart*.

The historic buildings along this stretch include the imposing Neoclassical **Custom House**, used for occasional public exhibitions and private events; the round **signal tower**, which was originally constructed as a windmill; and the turrets and towers of the **Sailors' Home**, built in Scots Baronial style in the 1880s as a dosshouse for seafarers.

Royal Yacht Britannia

MAP P.100, POCKET MAP A10
Ocean Terminal ☎ 0131 555 5566,
ⓦ royalyachtbritannia.co.uk. Daily: April–Sept 9.30am–4.30pm; Oct 9.30am–4pm; Nov–March 10am–3.30pm. £15.50.
Moored alongside **Ocean Terminal**, a huge shopping and entertainment centre designed by

Royal Yacht Britannia

Clydeside, Britannia was used by the royal family for 44 years for state visits, diplomatic functions and royal holidays. Leith acquired the vessel following decommission in 1997, against the wishes of many of the royal family, who felt that scuttling would have been a more dignified end. Alongside Britannia, the sleek former royal sailing yacht, Bloodhound, is also on view (Sept–June).

Visits to *Britannia* begin in the **visitor centre**, on the second floor of Ocean Terminal, where royal holiday snaps and video clips of the ship's most famous moments, which included the 1983 evacuation of Aden and the British handover of Hong Kong in 1997, are shown. An audio handset is then handed out and you're allowed to roam around the yacht: the **bridge**, the **engine room**, the **officers' mess** and a large part of the **state apartments**, including

Terence Conran, the **Royal Yacht Britannia** is one of the world's most famous ships. Launched in 1953 at John Brown's shipyard on

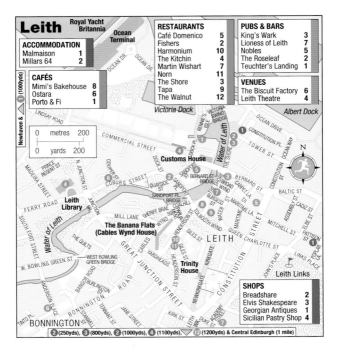

Leith — Royal Yacht Britannia — Ocean Terminal

ACCOMMODATION
Malmaison 1
Millars 64 2

CAFÉS
Mimi's Bakehouse 8
Ostara 6
Porto & Fi 1

RESTAURANTS
Café Domenico 5
Fishers 2
Harmonium 10
The Kitchin 4
Martin Wishart 7
Norn 11
The Shore 3
Tapa 9
The Walnut 12

PUBS & BARS
King's Wark 3
Lioness of Leith 7
Nobles 5
The Roseleaf 2
Teuchter's Landing 1

VENUES
The Biscuit Factory 6
Leith Theatre 4

SHOPS
Breadshare 2
Elvis Shakespeare 3
Georgian Antiques 1
Sicilian Pastry Shop 4

2 (250yds), 3 (800yds), 2 (1000yds), 4 (1100yds), ▽ 12 (1200yds) & Central Edinburgh (1 mile)

The Siege of Leith

In 1560 three thousand French troops found themselves caught up in a pivotal point in Scotland's history as the **Reformation** fuelled religious and political turmoil. The French had originally been asked to help protect Mary of Guise, Regent of Scotland, from the English in 1548, but Protestant Scots gradually turned against their protectors, coming to regard them more as occupiers than saviours. Skirmishes between the two sides began in 1559, with the heavily outnumbered but disciplined French soon gaining the upper hand. The Scots issued a request to England for help and for the first time in history the Scots would fight side by side with **"the Auld Enemy"**. Therein followed a period of unimaginable suffering as the French were ordered to defend their base in Leith "to the last of their blood and breath". Holed up within the town walls and with an English blockade of the port and cannonballs flying overhead, the French troops and Leith's townsfolk began to starve, reduced to eating cats, dogs and rats, according to contemporary accounts. The stalemate finally ended with Mary of Guise's death in June, 1560, and the signing of the **Treaty of Edinburgh** the following month, effectively ending the centuries-old **Auld Alliance** between Scotland and France.

the cabins used by the Queen and the Duke of Edinburgh. The ship has been kept largely as it was when in service, with a well-preserved 1950s dowdiness that the audio-guide loyally attributes to the Queen's good taste and astute frugality in the lean post-war years. Certainly, the atmosphere is a far cry from the opulent splendour that many expect.

Newhaven

The old village (now suburb) of **Newhaven** was established by James IV at the start of the sixteenth century as an alternative shipbuilding centre to Leith: his massive warship, the Great Michael – capable of carrying 120 gunners, three hundred mariners and a thousand troops, and said to have used up all the trees in Fife – was built here. Newhaven has also been a ferry station and an important fishing centre, landing some six million oysters a year at the height of its success in the 1860s. Today,

the chief pleasure is a stroll around the stone **harbour**, which still has a pleasantly salty feel, with a handful of boats tied up alongside or resting gently on the tidal mud.

Newhaven harbour

Shops

Breadshare

MAP P.100, POCKET MAP G1
4 Jane St ☎ 0131 538 4518,
ⓦ breadshare.co.uk. Tues & Thurs
10.30am–6pm, Wed, Fri & Sat
10.30am–3.30pm.

Award-winning community bakery
housed in a tiny side street shop
that uses stone ground flour and
slow fermentation techniques to
produce highly nutritious and
delicious loaves. Specializing in
organic and sourdough, they also
serve up a good range of takeaway
buns and sandwiches.

Elvis Shakespeare

MAP P.100, POCKET MAP G2
347 Leith Walk ☎ 0131 561 1363,
ⓦ elvisshakespeare.com. Mon–Sat
10am–6pm, May–Oct Sun noon–5pm.

Leith's favourite record and book
shop, specializing in second hand
literature and rare vinyl with a
subtle bias towards punk, post
punk and indie. The shop also hosts
regular live music sessions courtesy
of local artists.

Malteser slices at Mimi's Bakehouse

Georgian Antiques

MAP P.100, POCKET MAP C12
10 Pattison St ☎ 0131 553 7286,
ⓦ georgianantiques.net. Mon–Thurs
8.30am–5.30pm, Fri 8.30am–5pm, Sat
10am–2pm.

Enormous multi-tiered warehouse
bulging with antiquities small
and large. There's something for
everyone here with items ranging
from fine furniture and taxidermy
to old golf clubs and riding boots.

Sicilian Pastry Shop

MAP P.100, POCKET MAP F2
14–16 Albert St ☎ 0131 554 7417. Mon–Fri
8am–5pm, Sat 8am–4pm.

A brilliant little family shop selling
sweet and colourful cakes, mostly
Sicilian in style – featuring lots
of cream. Not really a café but
they do sell a nice, potent espresso
here, too.

Cafés

Mimi's Bakehouse

MAP P.100, POCKET MAP B11
63 Shore ☎ 0131 555 5908,
ⓦ mimisbakehouse.com. Mon–Fri
9am–5pm, Sat & Sun 9am–6pm.

Family-run, vintage-styled teashop;
its lovingly crafted cakes, tray
bakes and scones make for an
appetizingly colourful counter
display. The light lunches on offer
are a treat too, but best of all is
the tiered afternoon tea platter for
£16.50.

Ostara

MAP P.100, POCKET MAP B11
52 Coburg St ☎ 0131 261 5441,
ⓦ ostaracafe.co.uk. Daily 8am–4pm.

Brunch specialists serving up some
of the city's most vibrant plates
of food. There are lots of healthy
options on the menu like smashed
avocado on sourdough and fruity
porridge, while those in need of
an umami hit should target the
patatas bravas, mushroom salt,
smoky ketchup, halloumi and fried
egg for £8.

Porto & Fi

MAP P.100

47 Main St, Newhaven ☎ 0131 551 1900, ⓦ www.portofi.com. Mon–Thurs 8am–8pm, Fri & Sat 8am–10pm, Sun 10am–6pm.

A bright daytime/early-evening café-restaurant not far from Newhaven's old stone harbour, with tempting cakes and a seafood focused menu that includes fish pie and haddock kedgeree for £12 each.

Restaurants

Café Domenico

MAP P.100, POCKET MAP B11

30 Sandport St ☎ 0131 467 7266, ⓦ cafedomenico.co.uk. Mon–Thurs 10am–2.30pm & 5–10pm, Fri 10am–2.30pm & 5–10.30pm, Sat 10.30am–10.30pm, Sun 11am–10pm.

A superb value authentic backstreet Italian restaurant (not a café) that dishes up damn fine Italian fast food and take away sandwiches. Slurp down a spaghetti alle vongole for just £6.

Fishers

MAP P.100, POCKET MAP B11

1 Shore ☎ 0131 554 5666, ⓦ fishersrestaurants.co.uk. Mon–Sat noon–late, Sun 12.30pm–late.

Swanky fish bistro set in a seventeenth-century watchtower, Fishers helped to put Leith's dining scene on the map. The à la carte prices are pretty steep, like the £40 lobster, but you'll soon find your sea legs with the £15 set menu for two courses.

Harmonium

MAP P.100, POCKET MAP B12

60 Henderson St ☎ 0131 555 3160, ⓦ facebook.com/harmoniumbar. Daily noon–1am.

From the team behind Glasgow's famous music record shop/vegan café, *Mono*, Harmonium is pushing back the boundaries of the vegan cause with its cutting-edge gastro bar grub. Oysters, crab, caviar, quarter pounders and even black

Fishers

pudding feature on their menus – in interpretive plant form at least – and at lunch time specials are only a fiver.

The Kitchin

MAP P.100, POCKET MAP B11

78 Commercial Quay ☎ 0131 555 1755, ⓦ thekitchin.com. Tues–Sat noon–2.30pm & 6–9.30pm.

Opened in 2006 by celebrity chef Tom Kitchin and the winner – less than six months later – of a Michelin star, the motto here is "from nature to plate", a philosophy that ensures the freshest ingredients, particularly well demonstrated on their "Celebration of the Season" menu where you might find lobster with snail butter or grouse with girolles. Menus range from £33 (three course lunch) to £85 (five course Chef's Surprise Tasting menu).

Martin Wishart

MAP P.100, POCKET MAP B11

52 Shore ☎ 0131 553 3557, ⓦ restaurantmartinwishart.co.uk. Tues–Thurs noon–1.30pm & 7–9pm, Fri –Sat noon–1.30pm & 6.30–9.30pm.

The eponymous chef is one of the leading lights of the Scottish

Norn

culinary scene, and was the first Michelin-star holder in Edinburgh. Expect highly accomplished and exquisitely presented dishes featuring Scottish-sourced fish and meat. A two-course lunch (Tues–Fri) is £32 while a six-course evening tasting menu costs £85.

Norn

MAP P.100, POCKET MAP B12
50–54 Henderson St ☏ 0131 629 2525,
Ⓦ nornrestaurant.com. Tues–Wed 7pm to late, Thurs–Say 5.30pm–late.
Set to give its Michelin-starred neighbours a good run for their money, Leith's newest and most exciting fine dining restaurant takes the best of Scotland's larder – foraged, farmed and fished; whatever comes in that day – and delivers some of the most creative, confident plates you're ever likely to encounter. There's no menu, just choose either four or seven courses (£40 and £60 respectively) and book well ahead. Past glories have included asparagus with pea and sorrel purée and veal topside with St George mushrooms and chicken stock gravy.

The Shore

MAP P.100, POCKET MAP B11
3–4 Shore ☏ 0131 553 5080,
Ⓦ fishersrestaurants.co.uk. Mon–Sat noon–late, Sun 12.30pm–late.

Well-lived-in bar-restaurant with huge mirrors, wood panelling and aproned waiters who serve up good sea (and land) food from £13.50. Live jazz, folk and general hubbub float through from the adjoining bar where you'll find a wide selection of snacks on offer, including trout and herb croquettes for £4.50.

Tapa

MAP P.100, POCKET MAP B12
19 Shore Place ☏ 0131 476 6776,
Ⓦ tapaedinburgh.co.uk. Tues–Thurs noon–11pm, Fri & Sat noon–midnight.
Authentic Spanish restaurant in an attractive old warehouse offering good value tapas and a superb sherry list. The £15 for two people lunch deal is a bargain and includes the standout tapa, aubergine crisp with honey.

The Walnut

MAP P.100, POCKET MAP F2
9 Croall Place, Leith Walk ☏ 0131 281 1236. Mon–Fri noon–2.30pm & 6–9.30pm, Sat & Sun noon–10pm.
One of Leith Walk's most popular neighbourhood diners thanks to its affordable, solid home-style British cooking and its bring your own bottle policy. A leek and potato tart and a steamed ginger pudding will set you back a mere tenner.

Pubs and Bars

Kings Wark

MAP P.100, POCKET MAP B11
36 Shore ☏ 0131 554 9260, Ⓦ kingswark. co.uk. Sun–Thurs 10am–midnight, Fri & Sat 10am–1am.
Restored fifteenth-century harbour side pub with attached restaurant. Its picturesque interior of stone walls and corniced ceilings gives an ambience that's changed very little since the days of the old sea dogs telling tales at the bar.

Lioness of Leith

MAP P.100, POCKET MAP B12
21–25 Duke St ☏ 0131 629 0580,

Ⓦ **thelionessofleith.co.uk**. Mon–Thurs noon–1am, Fri–Sun 11am–1am.

With pop art on the walls, an arcade machine in the corner and a table made out of a pinball machine, this Victorian boozer certainly looks young for its age. There's regular live music at weekends, a good kitchen and a loyal local following.

Nobles

MAP P.100, POCKET MAP C11
44a Constitution St Ⓣ 0131 629 7215,
Ⓦ **noblesbarleith.co.uk**. Mon–Wed 11am–midnight, Thurs & Fri 11am–1am, Sat & Sun 10am–1am.

Handsome Victorian bar with more than its fair share of stained glass, chandeliers and wood panelling, this is a good place to sup a posh cocktail or two. The bar's kitchen operates in gastro pub territory with a particularly fine dessert to look out for: green tea panna cotta with poached rhubarb for £7.

The Roseleaf

MAP P.100, POCKET MAP B11
23–24 Sandport Place Ⓣ 0131 476 5268,
Ⓦ **roseleaf.co.uk**. Daily 10am–1am.

Chintzy-cool local that's a little off the beaten track but worth the trip for the pot-tails alone – funky cocktails like the "Breakfast Club" (Finnish vodka with elderflower, mint and citrus fruits) served in vintage teapots at around £10 for two people.

Teuchter's Landing

MAP P.100, POCKET MAP B11
1 Dock Place Ⓣ 0131 554 7427,
Ⓦ **teuchtersbar.co.uk**. Daily 10.30am–1am.

Spilling out onto a bespoke pontoon, with seductive harbour views, Teuchter's beer garden is the ideal place to while away a braw, bricht summer's afternoon. The pub itself, converted from a waiting room for the decommissioned Leith to Aberdeen steamboat, is a delightful, traditional style free house dissected into a genial collection of nooks and snugs

with an overcrowded bar and a superfluously large whisky selection.

Venues

The Biscuit Factory

MAP P.100, POCKET MAP A12
4–6 Anderson Place Ⓣ 0131 629 0809,
Ⓦ **biscuitfactory.co.uk**.

Arts and fashion venue in an old industrial estate warehouse. Besides the workshops and gin distillery, the building hosts an eclectic range of events including late night warehouse parties, monthly food and craft markets, beer and music festivals and interesting pop up restaurants.

Leith Theatre

MAP P.100, POCKET MAP A11
28–30 Ferry Road Ⓣ 0131 629 0810,
Ⓦ **leiththeatretrust.org**

Undergoing a staggered refurbishment after three decades of abandonment, this delightful Art Deco auditorium is beginning to reopen its doors again. Having successfully hosted the Hidden Door Festival (see page 144), more art and live music performances will be on the cards.

Teuchter's Landing

West Edinburgh

Suburban west Edinburgh has its own fair share of touristic temptations, chiefly that of the enormous zoo that covers a good tranche of Corstorphine Hill's southern slopes and Murrayfield Stadium, home of the Scottish rugby team. There's also much history to be discovered here among the ancient satellite villages since subsumed by the city's exponential growth in the last century. The old Roman settlement of Cramond has a familiar seaside town feel to it, while just inland, Lauriston Castle is one of only a handful still standing within the city limits. Chimneys still pierce the skyline, frequently delivering west Edinburgh's characteristic malty aroma; a reminder of the city's brewing heritage originally powered by the coal delivered along the Union Canal and the railways that criss-cross the landscape.

Edinburgh Zoo

MAP P.107
134 Corstorphine Rd ☎ 0131 334 9171,
ⓦ edinburghzoo.org.uk. Daily: April–Sept
9am–6pm; March & Oct 9am–5pm;
Nov–Feb 9am–4.30pm. Adults & children
£17 & £12.50 in advance, £19 & £14.55
on the door. Penguin parade daily 2.15pm

Jaguar at Edinburgh Zoo

April–Sept, and sunny days March & Oct.
Buses #12, #26 & #31 westbound from
Princes Street.

Set on an eighty-acre site on the slopes of Corstorphine Hill, **Edinburgh Zoo** has transformed itself in recent years into a modern conservation and recreation park success and one of the city's must-see attractions. Appealingly set in the midst of a botanic garden, the new enclosures offer plenty of opportunities for up-close animal encounters and the heralded arrival of giant pandas in 2011 has bolstered the zoo's already impressive collection. Spaces to see the pandas are extremely limited on busy days so it's advisable to book your free slot a day or two earlier. Beyond the pandas it's a bit of an uphill hike to the far end of the zoo but once there you can admire the city views, then wander back down passing under the reinforced glass tiger tunnel, past the Asiatic lions and sun bears, and arrive at the enormous dedicated chimpanzee research centre. Unless it's raining, the place is permanently packed with kids, and the zoo's most famous attraction for youngsters is its **penguin parade**, when rangers entice a waddle of the flightless birds to leave their enclosure for a short circuit lined with admiring spectators.

Murrayfield Stadium

MAP P.107
West Stand, Roseburn St ☎ 0131 346 5106, ⓦ scottishrugby.org/murrayfield-stadium/tours. Stadium tours Mon–Sat 11am & Thurs–Fri 2.30pm, 9mins, guided. £10.

The home of Scottish rugby since 1925 when, on its **Murrayfield** debut, the home side scraped a narrow win over England in front of seventy thousand spectators. Although similar successes are rather thin on the ground these days, today's modern panorama-hogging stadium – the largest in Scotland – must still be an intimidating prospect for the biannual visitors from south of the border. To witness the place from the players point of view join one

Six Nations rugby match at Murrayfield

of the regular tours that focus on the inner workings of the stadium with a ninety minute anecdote-laden exposure to the commentary box, dressing room and trophy cabinets. The highlight of the visit

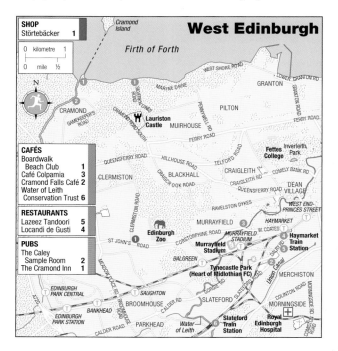

West Edinburgh

SHOP	
Störtebäcker	1

Cramond Island
Firth of Forth

CAFÉS	
Boardwalk Beach Club	1
Café Colpamia	3
Cramond Falls Café	2
Water of Leith Conservation Trust	6

RESTAURANTS	
Lazeez Tandoori	5
Locandi de Gusti	4

PUBS	
The Caley Sample Room	2
The Cramond Inn	1

Lauriston Castle

is unquestionably the trot out onto the pitch through the tunnel to the imagined roar of a capacity crowd.

Lauriston Castle

MAP P.107

2a Cramond Rd South ☎ 0131 336 2060, Ⓦ edinburghmuseums.org.uk. Guided tours: April–Oct Sat–Thurs 2pm, Nov–March Sat & Sun 2pm. Gardens April–Sept 9am–8pm, Oct–March 9am–5pm. House £5, Gardens free. Bus no.41 westbound from Princes Street.

A short walk from the popular seaside settlement of Cramond, this sixteenth-century tower house with Jacobean style extensions still looks the part in its rural parkland setting. Its north face gazes out across the croquet lawn to the choppy Firth of Forth, while respite from a bitter northerly can be found in the delightful adjacent Japanese walled garden.

Approached from its southern flank across a large meadow, the building itself is most interesting for its interior. Bequeathed in 1926 to Edinburgh council under the strict proviso that it remained unchanged, the building gives a rare and charming insight into a lived-in Edwardian-Scottish country pile.

Cramond

MAP P.107

5 miles northwest of the town centre. Bus #41 westbound from central Princes Street. For tide times, either check the noticeboard on shore or look for tide times for Leith on the Ⓦ bbc.co.uk/weather.

The enduring image of **Cramond** is of step-gabled whitewashed houses rising uphill from the waterfront, though it also has the foundations of a Roman fort, and a tower house, church, inn and mansion, all from the seventeenth century. The best reason to come here is to enjoy a stroll around and a bit of fresh air. The **walk** along the wide promenade that follows the shoreline offers great views of the Forth; or head out across the causeway to the uninhabited bird sanctuary of Cramond Island – though beware that the causeway disappears as high tide approaches and can leave you stranded if you get your timings wrong. Aim to get to and from the island in the two hours either side of low tide.

Inland of Cramond, there's another pleasant walk along a tree-lined path by the River Almond, past former mills and their adjoining cottages towards the sixteenth-century Old Cramond Bridge.

Canal boat trips

Surely the best way to experience the Union Canal is to take to the water by way of a boat trip; there are a few companies along the stretch that offer excursions and even boat hire. If you have the means, head out of town to Linlithgow where the trips include a crossing of the Avon aqueduct, the longest and tallest in Scotland, while Edinburgh's own trips are all about watching the city slip by over a leisurely cream tea.

LINLITHGOW CANAL CENTRE
Manse Road Basin ☎ 01506 671 215, Ⓦ lucs.org.uk. Town cruises: July to mid-Aug daily & April–Sept weekends 2–4.30pm; 25min. £4. Aqueduct cruises: Mid-April to Sept Sat & Sun 2pm; 2hr 30min. £8.

RE-UNION CANAL BOATS
MAP P.107
Fountainbridge ☎ 0131 261 8529, Ⓦ re-union.org.uk. Afternoon tea cruise (occasional) Sun 2pm; 2hr. £22.50.

From here you can either continue upstream or cross the bridge and head back towards the coast within the grounds of Dalmeny Estate, where there are wonderful little-known beaches and forest walks as well as a stately home – Dalmeny House (see page 123) and the evocative baronial-style Barnbougle Castle alone on the water's edge.

Union Canal
MAP P.107
Begins at Fountainbridge, a short walk west of the centre.
Like an environmental lance, the **Union Canal** pierces deep into the heart of formerly industrialized west-central Edinburgh, bringing with it a perfect bike friendly opportunity to escape the confines of the city away from traffic. Passing wildfowl, barges and lofty viaducts, the route swiftly shifts through the city's suburbs before breaking out into delightful tree enclosed countryside en-route to Falkirk, home of the Kelpies – thirty-metre-tall metallic horse head sculptures – and the Falkirk wheel, a unique engineering feat that lifts barges between the Union, Forth and Clyde canals.

Originally built in 1822, the canal was an important artery for the industrial revolution, delivering coal to power Falkirk's iron casting works and Edinburgh's many breweries as well as to heat the swelling number of residential houses in the capital. Just two decades after its opening, the construction of railways in the area dealt a hammer blow to its prosperity and the canal went into a near terminal spiral of decline stopped in its tracks in recent years by a reflective political will to protect Scotland's heritage and fragile ecosystems.

A barge on the Union Canal

Edinburgh for Kids

Look at a map of town and it's pleasingly evident that Edinburgh's green belt makes up more than half the city's acreage. With its seven hills, forests, river, canal and coastal paths and interconnecting network of dedicated cycle paths, Edinburgh is the ideal place for children to experience the great outdoors with the benefits of an urban environment close at hand. When the weather's against you, there's a large number of child-friendly attractions in which to seek refuge, many of which are free.

Top 5 things to do on a rainy day

MUSEUM OF SCOTLAND
(See page 51)
Cavernous and interactive, the Museum of Scotland is a perfect spot for kids to play games, dig for fossils and program robots, while for little tots there's a colourful sensory room befit with musical stepping stones, a Wendy house, and shadow puppets.

OUR DYNAMIC EARTH
(See page 61)
Subterranean, family-friendly exploration into the geology of our planet with numerous interactive exhibits, an earthquake simulation and a 4D cinema finale.

CAMERA OBSCURA & WORLD OF ILLUSIONS
(See page 32)
A city favourite for kids of all ages with floor after floor of holograms, optical illusions, mirrors and hands on exhibits.

EICA CLIP AND CLIMB
(See page 121)
At the enormous climbing centre just west of Edinburgh, Clip and Climb is a series of challenges designed for children (4 years and over) that includes climbing walls, huge spheres and tubes to scale as well as jumps and slides.

EDINBURGH DUNGEON
(See page 67)
One for older kids, Edinburgh Dungeon seeks to simultaneously scare and entertain with spine-chilling rides and talking severed heads that take you on a journey into Edinburgh's gruesome medieval past.

Top 3 fair weather things to do with kids

EDINBURGH ZOO
(See page 106)
Pandas, parks and penguin parades; Edinburgh Zoo is the number one child-friendly destination in town.

GORGIE CITY FARM
MAP P.107
51 Gorgie Rd ☎ 0131 337 4202, ⓦ gorgiecityfarm.org.uk. Daily summer 9.30am–4.30pm, winter 9.30am–4pm. Free, donations welcomed.
It couldn't be in a more unlikely setting, but this volunteer-run working farm brings the countryside into the urban. Kids can pet the animals, feed the ruminants and admire the cockerels before taking to the wheel of a static tractor.

MIDLOTHIAN SNOWSPORTS CENTRE
Biggar Rd, Hillend ☎ 0131 445 4433, ⓦ midlothian.gov.uk/info/200281/snowsports_centre. Mon–Fri 10am–9pm, Sat & Sun 9.30am–7pm. Tubing adults £10.20, children £8.20. Take the no.15 bus from Waverley Bridge.
This winter sports centre lies just outside the city boundary on the northernmost slopes of the Pentland hills. Kids will love jumping into a tyre and hurling themselves down the slippery slopes at uncomfortably fast speeds. As well as tubing, there's a decently precipitous dry slope for all year skiing and boarding.

THE YARD
(See page 93)
Brilliant organic adventure playground made out of reclaimed junk; designed by the BBC's *DIY SOS* programme for carefree play.

PORTOBELLO BEACH
(See page 63)
Good old fashioned British beach resort with golden sands, play parks, a promenade and fish and chips.

Shop

Störtebäcker

MAP P.107

38 St John's Rd ⊕ 07752 186 564,
ⓦ stortebacker.co.uk. Tues, Wed, Fri & Sat
9am–2pm.

Surely the world's smallest bakery, housed in the "wee shop" with standing room for just two people plus a veritable bounty of outstanding home-made (literally) sourdoughs, cakes, pastries and tarts. Loosely translated as "harassed baker", this enterprise is the brainchild of two German friends with a passion for the *torten* and *brot* of home.

Cafés

Boardwalk Beach Club

MAP P.107

50 Marine Drive, Silverknowes
⊕ 0131 336 2661, ⓦ facebook.com/
boardwalkbeachclub. Wed–Fri 9.30am–
5pm, Sat & Sun 9.30am–6pm; closes at
dusk in winter.

Unique standalone café with unhindered sea views and a clientele that ebbs and flows depending on the weather; chairs spill out beyond the patio to the

Boardwalk Beach Club

lawn on those rare balmy summer days. There's nothing surprising on the menu – panini, soup, cake et al – but it's the quality of the food and drink that would make this place stand out from the competition, if there was any.

Café Colpamia

MAP P.107

8 Murrayfield Place ⊕ 0131 337 2492. Mon
8.30am–5pm, Tues–Fri 8.30am–8pm, Sat
10am–5pm.

A short walk from the Modern Art galleries and Murrayfield Stadium, this café-bistro offers an authentic taste of Palermo with their home-made torta, biscotti, zuppa and bruschetta. Wash them down with a fine cappuccino or a glass of Sicilian wine.

Cramond Falls Café

MAP P.107

10 School Brae ⊕ 0131 312 8408,
ⓦ cramondfalls.co.uk. July & Aug Mon–Fri
10am–5pm, Sat & Sun 10am–5.30pm, Sept–
June Mon, Tues, Thurs & Fri 10am–4pm, Sat
& Sun 10am–5.30pm, closed Dec.

Taking its name from the delightful adjacent waterfall, this café, converted from a seventeenth century mill, makes for an idyllic distraction on a saunter up Cramond's River Almond. You can have a hearty

cooked breakfast here or a freshly baked scone – if you time it right and there are plenty of health-conscious and veggie options, too.

Water of Leith Conservation Trust

MAP P.107

24 Lanark Rd ☎ 0131 455 7367, ⓦ waterofleith.org.uk. Daily 10am–4pm.
An almost compulsory stop if you're walking the Water of Leith. Dunk a couple of biscuits in a pleasingly cheap cuppa then have a quick browse around the small, free exhibition on the river's wildlife and industrial heritage that includes a child-friendly "interactive zone".

Restaurants

Lazeez Tandoori

MAP P.107, POCKET MAP A6

191 Dalry Rd ☎ 0131 337 7977, ⓦ lazeeztandoori.co.uk. Mon & Wed–Sat 4pm–midnight, Sun 5pm–midnight.
Cunningly disguised as an insalubrious kebab joint, Lazeez defies all presuppositions with its sensational Punjabi home-style cooking; among the best in town with plenty of heat. The homemade *kheer* (Indian rice pudding) – the result of twelve hours of cooking – is light, delicious and necessarily cleansing. Mains hover around the £6.50 mark.

Locanda De Gusti

MAP P.107, POCKET MAP B6

102 Dalry Rd ☎ 0131 346 8800, ⓦ locandadegusti.com. Mon–Sat 5.30–10pm & Thurs–Sat 12.30–2pm.
Brought up in a large Neapolitan family, owner Rosario Sartore knows his cipollas when it comes to true Italian home cooking. Kitted out like a modern day osteria, the colourful décor is outshone by the vibrancy of the food. Grilled seafood is usually the star of the show here while the homemade egg pasta courses for around £10 – including the gluten free ones – are light and deliciously garlicky.

The Caley Sample Room

Pubs

The Caley Sample Room

MAP P.107, POCKET MAP A7

42–58 Angle Park Terrace ☎ 0131 337 7204, ⓦ thecaleysampleroom.co.uk. Mon–Thurs noon–midnight, Fri noon–1am, Sat 10am–1am, Sun 10am–midnight.
Named after, although not affiliated to, Edinburgh's oldest surviving brewery, The Caledonian (sited in the delightful Victorian factory nearby), this pub-restaurant proudly reserves a tap for its namesake's famous Deuchar's IPA. If that's not for your pallet then there's a feast of guest taps that change daily and bottled ales to cheer the dourest CAMRA inspector. The pub also has a good rep for homemade gastropub grub with set menus starting at £12.

The Cramond Inn

MAP P.107

30 Cramond Glebe Rd ☎ 0131 336 2035. Mon–Thurs 11am–11pm; Fri & Sat 11am–midnight; Sun 12.30–11pm.
A proper village local with coal fires for nippy days and a sea view beer garden for temperate ones. Owners Samuel Smith, Yorkshire's oldest brewery, provide the wide range of beers.

South Edinburgh

Stubbornly middle class, leafy and Labour-voting, the political constituency of Edinburgh South encompasses some of the city's most desirable and cosmopolitan postcodes including Newington, Marchmont, Bruntsfield and Morningside. Fringed and softened by the green expanse of the Meadows, Newington and Marchmont have long been home to a vibrant, multinational mix of well-off students and young families while Bruntsfield, with its vintage furniture shops and Farrow and Ball-painted brunch spots, stakes its claim as the Hampstead of the north. House prices rise even further as the latter morphs into the mansions of archetypally genteel Morningside. There aren't many sights as such, though you can easily lose yourself amid the trails of Blackford Hill Nature Reserve and – at least in winter – go stargazing in the Royal Observatory. The real pleasure here is simply wandering at will, following your nose among the pungent aromas of artisan coffee and cheese shops, bakeries and bistros.

Newington

MAP P.116, POCKET MAP G7

Blending into the city's grittier Southside in the lee of Salisbury Crags at one end, and stretching out to the handsome Victorian townhouses of the Grange at the other, **Newington** is predominantly young, always buzzing and ever changing. Home to the bulk of

Edinburgh University halls, Newington

Edinburgh University and its huge and multi-ethnic academic population, the area has seen swanky student accommodation blocks mushroom in recent years, with an ever-expanding array of shops, bars, cafés and restaurants. Newington is likewise the epicentre of the **Fringe** come August, home to both the Pleasance Courtyard and Assembly Roxy, and with the Gilded Balloon, Pleasance Dome and Underbelly all setting up temporary shop and swelling the youthful population even further. Multi-arts venue Summerhall (see page 119), meanwhile, is both a festival uber-hub and a year-round hipster fixture, the most exciting addition to Edinburgh's arts scene in years.

The Meadows

MAP P.116, POCKET MAP E6

An elm-lined, fan-shaped park tracing the boundaries of Newington, Marchmont and

Cherry blossom in The Meadows

Tollcross, **The Meadows** – like Princes Street Gardens – began life as a loch, in this case supplying much of Edinburgh's drinking water. At the instigation of Sir Thomas Hope it was drained in the eighteenth century and a law passed in 1827 forbidding construction on the site. The classic **urban park** that emerged is a joy: criss-crossed by cycle and pedestrian paths and bordered by assorted food trucks, kiosks and cafés, it comes into its own in spring and summer when people flock here from nearby tenements for impromptu barbecues, games of cricket and al fresco prosecco. With the background thrum of djembe drums, the waft of sizzling veggie burgers and a babylon of voices it has a much more bohemian vibe than Princes Street Gardens, and often akin to a low-key music festival. Unsurprisingly, its often at its busiest in August with various tented venues springing up and festival goers basking in the sun.

Bruntsfield and Morningside

MAP P.116, POCKET MAP C8
Bus #5, #11, #15, #16, #23 or #36

To the southwest of the Meadows, **Bruntsfield Links** is the only remnant of the old Burgh Muir, an ancient five-square-mile expanse of grazing land with a chequered history including use as a hanging ground and quarantine area for plague victims. To the west of the Links is **Bruntsfield** itself, a wealthy enclave populated by independent shops, cafés and restaurants, and no stranger to the big screen, appearing in both *The Prime of Miss Jean Brodie* and, more recently, *Trainspotting T2*. Past the final curve of Bruntsfield Place, the ancient thoroughfare of Morningside Road climbs dead south into one of Edinburgh's (and Scotland's) wealthiest, most satirised and – according to a recent survey – happiest suburbs. Famous as the fictional home of the aforementioned Miss Jean Brodie, **Morningside** only occasionally lives up to the clichés. While the surrounding streets are home to all manner of eye-poppingly expensive Victorian confections, Morningside Road itself is lined with tenements and has a surprisingly down to earth feel; a friendly, bustling mix of bistros, artisan food outlets

Morningside

and antique-filled charity shops, plus the iconic and infamously intimidating Canny Man's pub (see page 119). Don't miss the late Art Deco splendour of the Dominion Cinema on Newbattle Terrace, by far the most luxurious place in Edinburgh to catch a film; the velvet-lined lobbies are filled with pre-selfie photographic portraits of visiting stars.

The Hermitage of Braid and Blackford Hill Local Nature Reserve

MAP P.116
Braid Road ☏ 0131 529 2401, ⓦ edinburgh.gov.uk. Hermitage House Visitor Centre Mon–Fri 9am–4pm. Bus #11 or #15

Way off the tourist trail and probably all the better for it, this wonderful, ancient woodland-designated **nature reserve** is accessible from Braid Road on the southern fringes of Morningside. The near 150-acre site is at its most dramatic around the steep gorge that slices through the **Hermitage of Braid**, with paths threading across precipitous slopes covered in mature elm, ash, beech, sycamore, rowan and oak, themselves some of the city's tallest trees. **Hermitage House** nestles in glorious seclusion among

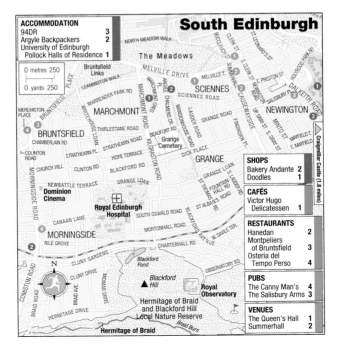

them in the middle of the glen, accessed by a tarmac drive. Built in 1785 by local architect Robert Burn, its castellated Gothic revival stylings would be echoed in turn by Burn's son, William, one of the pioneers of the Scots Baronial style. Today the Hermitage is category A-listed and home to a **Visitor Centre**, where you can pick up maps for the reserve's orienteering course. Nearby is a formerly derelict **walled garden** and extravagant **doocot** (dovecot), originally built to supply a long-gone fortified castle. Once containing almost 2000 sandstone nest boxes, the doocot presumably satisfied what must have been one almighty appetite for pigeon pie. Myriad volunteer groups, meanwhile, have transformed the walled land into a **community wildlife garden** in recent years, a work in progress geared towards wildflowers and native medicinal plants. To the west paths lead to the wide-open spaces of **Blackford Hill**, with magnificent views north over the cityscape and south to the Pentland and Moorfoot Hills.

Royal Observatory

MAP P.116

Blackford Hill ⓣ 0131 668 8404, ⓦ roe.ac.uk. Astronomy evenings May–Sept monthly Fri 7.30–9pm (see website for dates); Oct–April weekly Fri 6.30–7.30pm & 8–9pm; online pre-booking only. £5. Bus #24 or #41

While Scotland is now at the forefront of space science and satellite technology, Edinburgh's **Royal Observatory** has been scanning the heavens from its prime position on Blackford Hill since 1896. Recognised worldwide for its contributions to, and development of, astronomy, the Observatory is also one of the architectural landmarks of south Edinburgh, its distinctive form bookended by octagonal towers supporting copper-sheathed, cylindrical telescope housing. Their **Astronomy Evenings** take in the original **Victorian telescope**

dome and in winter, weather depending, you'll witness the firmament like you've never seen it before. Note that tours are held on a strictly pre-booked basis and demand is higher in winter when it's best to book well in advance.

Craigmillar Castle

MAP P.116

Craigmillar Castle Road ⓣ 0131 661 4445, ⓦ historicenvironment.scot. April–Sept daily 9.30am–5.30pm; Oct–March Mon–Wed, Sat & Sun 10am–4pm. £6. HES. Bus #8, #33 or #49

Craigmillar Castle sits amid a small tranche of green belt some five miles south of the city centre, offering an atmospheric, untrammelled contrast to packed Edinburgh Castle. The oldest part of the complex is the **L-shaped tower house**, which dates back to the early 1400s – this remains substantially intact, and the **great hall**, with its resplendent late Gothic chimneypiece, is in good enough shape to be rented out for functions. Once occasionally used by Mary, Queen of Scots the **tower house**, however, was abandoned to its picturesque decay in the mid-eighteenth century.

Royal Observatory

Shops

Bakery Andante

MAP P.116, POCKET MAP C9
352 Morningside Rd ☎ 0131 447 8473,
ⓦ bakeryandante.co.uk. Mon–Sat
7.30am–6pm, Sun 8.30am–1pm. Bus #5,
#11, #15, #16, #23 or #36

Award-winning artisan bakery
selling a range of delicious
sourdough breads, none more so
than their unsurpassably crusty
Covenanter. The almond croissants
are just as heavenly. This kind of
quality doesn't come cheap but look
out for morning bargains in the
shape of half-price, still-fresh loaves
unsold from the previous day.

Doodles

MAP P.116, POCKET MAP E7
29 Marchmont Crescent ☎ 0131 229
1399, ⓦ doodlesscotland.co.uk. Mon,
Fri & Sat 10am–6pm, Tues, Wed & Thurs
10.30am–9pm, Sun noon–6pm. Bus #5,
#24 or #41

Edinburgh's original and best paint-
your-own pottery workshop. If you
have kids in tow and you're going
to be in town for more than 4/5
days (the time it takes to glaze and
fire your masterpiece), this is a great
rainy-day diversion. See the website
for inspiration.

Café

Victor Hugo Delicatessen

MAP P.116, POCKET MAP E7
26–27 Melville Terrace, Marchmont
☎ 0131 667 1827, ⓦ victorhugodeli.com.
Mon–Fri 8am–8pm, Sat & Sun 8am–6pm.

Even on the darkest and coldest of
winter days, locals huddle around
the gingham-clad outdoor tables
of this Meadows-Marchmont
landmark. In business since
WWII, the place has recently been
refurbished, though the famous
black and scarlet exterior, and deli
classics – think eggs benedict and
pastrami on rye – remain.

Montpeliers of Bruntsfield

Restaurants

Hanedan

MAP P.116, POCKET MAP F7
41 West Preston Street, Newington ☎ 0131
667 4242, ⓦ hanedan.co.uk. Tues–Sun
noon–3pm & 5.30pm–late.

With only twelve tables, this tiny
box of Turkish delights doesn't
take long to fill up. Décor couldn't
be less pretentious, and the food
follows suit: rich, salty moussaka is
arguably the best in the city, while
their marinated chicken and lamb
melts in the mouth; the moist,
nutty baklava simply sticks to it.
Mains £10–12.

Montpeliers of Bruntsfield

MAP P.116, POCKET MAP C8
159–161 Bruntsfield Place ☎ 0131 229
3115, ⓦ montpeliersedinburgh.co.uk. Daily
9am–1am. Bus #11, #15, #16, #23 or #36.

The well-manicured pillar of
Bruntsfield's dining establishment,
and a rare constant in Edinburgh's
formidable turnover of bars and
restaurants. You'll likely need to
book if you want to enjoy one of
their famous trad brunches (£5–10)
or well-regarded mains (£10–15);

try the pan-fired sea bass on sprouting broccoli.

Osteria del Tempo Perso

MAP P.116, POCKET MAP C8

208 Bruntsfield Place ⓣ 0131 221 1777, ⓦ osteriadeltempoperso.info. Jan–July & Sept–Nov Mon–Thurs noon–2.30pm & 5pm–late, Fri–Sun noon–late; Aug & Dec daily noon–late. Bus #11, #15, #16, #23 or #36

The Bruntsfield *bambino* of a Lazio-based papa, this family-run affair is a more authentic Italian experience than many. A dazzling mosaic-tiled ceiling, inimitably informal service, ravishingly garlicky pasta and a better-than-moussaka parmigiana di melanzane are all testament to *the* proverbial *dolce vita*. Mains £10–15.

Pubs

The Canny Man's

MAP P.116, POCKET MAP C9

239 Morningside Rd ⓣ 0131 447 1484, ⓦ cannymans.co.uk. Mon–Wed & Sun 11am–11pm, Thurs & Sat 11pm–midnight, Fri 11am–1am. Bus #5, #11, #15, #16, #23 or #36

More Churchillian time capsule than pub and an exquisite – if often frostily exclusive – antidote to Edinburgh's interior design arms race; even the dust used to be antique. "The best pub in the world" according to Rick Stein, and he might not be far off. Just don't necessarily expect a warm welcome.

The Salisbury Arms

MAP P.116, POCKET MAP G7

58 Dalkeith Road, Newington ⓣ 0131 667 4518, ⓦ thesalisburyarmsedinburgh.co.uk. Mon–Thurs 11am–11pm, Fri & Sat 11am–midnight, Sun noon–11pm

A gorgeous Victorian town house set comfortably back from busy Dalkeith Road, this countrified gastropub is perfect for a post-Arthur's Seat pint. The leafy, partially secluded beer garden is one of Edinburgh's hidden delights, while a roaring fire, decent mains (£10–15) and pleasant staff make for an inviting interior.

Venues

The Queens Hall

MAP P.116, POCKET MAP E7

85–89 Clerk Street, Newington ⓣ 0131 668 2019, ⓦ thequeenshall.net.

There's nothing quite like an intimate jazz or classical performance in the hushed environs of this former church, one of Edinburgh's best loved live music venues. Also stages folk and world music, plus the odd pop and rock gig. Comes into its own during the Fringe.

Summerhall

MAP P.116, POCKET MAP E7

Summerhall Square, Newington ⓣ 0131 560 1580, ⓦ summerhall.co.uk. The Royal Dick Mon–Sat noon–late, Sat & Sun noon–1am.

Edinburgh's largest and most ambitious multi-discipline arts, artisan and tech hub – everything from cutting edge theatre to craft brewing, live music to club nights; check the website for upcoming events. The onsite *Royal Dick* bar reflects Summerhall's previous incarnation as a veterinary school, replete with specimen cases, microscopes and animal bones.

Summerhall

Day Trips

Cast your line just beyond Edinburgh's tight margins and you'll bear witness to tantalising glimpses of what the mother country has to offer. Castles, abbeys and stately homes in various stages of decay perforate a landscape of verdant valleys, bleak hill farms and rugged coastline on a virtual par with anything Scotland has to offer. The capital boasts some cracking new satellite attractions too including the vast indoor climbing centre at Ratho and the boat lifting engineering marvel that is the Falkirk Wheel while the large sculpture park at Jupiter Artland is an unexpected highlight of the region's irrepressible art scene.

South Queensferry and the Forth Bridges

MAP P.122

8 miles northwest of Edinburgh city centre. From Edinburgh Waverley take the bi-hourly train to Dalmeny. From there it's just under a mile to town, west on Station Road then turn right on The Loan.

Best known today for its location at the southern end of three mighty **Forth Bridges** the small town of **South Queensferry** is an attractive old settlement with its narrow, cobbled High Street

Forth Rail Bridge

lined with tightly packed old buildings. Through a gap there's a great perspective of the Forth Bridges from the old stone harbour and curved, pebbly beach – the scene each New Year's Day of the teeth-chattering "Loony Dook", when a gaggle of hungover locals charge into the sea for the sharpest of dips.

While the final death knell for the ferry service from here to Fife – that had run from the eleventh century – rang on the opening of the first road bridge, there's still much local pride in the crossings that form the unavoidable backdrop to this town as evidenced in the local museum on the High Street that detail their construction.

The bridges themselves, erected across three separate centuries, were each pioneering in their own right. The cantilevered **Forth Rail Bridge**, built from 1883 to 1890, ranks among the supreme achievements of Victorian engineering. Some fifty thousand tons of steel were used in the construction of a design that manages to express grace as well as might.

Its neighbour, the **Forth Road Bridge** was the fourth largest suspension bridge in the world

Weeping Girl by Laura Ford at Jupiter Artland

on its completion in 1964. A combination of its gradual decay and the increased volumes of traffic led to the decision to build a new road bridge a little further to the west.

Opened in 2017, **Queensferry Crossing** – the world's longest cable stayed bridge – with its white symmetrical cables gracefully fanning out from a trio of towers to the deck below, is as much admired for its restrained beauty as its engineering prowess.

The best way to admire all three engineering feats at once is to make use of the pedestrian and cycle lane on the Forth Road Bridge.

Jupiter Artland

MAP P.122
Wilkieston, 11 miles west of Edinburgh on the B7015 ☎ 01506 889 900, Ⓦ jupiter artland.org. May–July & Sept Thurs–Sun 10am–5pm, July–Aug daily 10am–5pm. £8.50. Bus #27 from Princes Street.
Fulfilling the dreams of its art collector owners, this one-hundred-acre country pile has been transformed since the turn of the century into the remarkable sculpture park **Jupiter Artland**. Its appeal as a virgin project, an unparalleled blank canvas, has drawn in many of the heavyweights of outdoor installation like Charles Jencks, whose signature swirling grassy hillocks and ponds also feature outside the Edinburgh's Modern Art Gallery. Here his landscape entitled "Cells of Life" interprets the biological process of mitosis using large grassy walnut whip-shaped mounds dissected by a drivable causeway. Andy Goldsworthy contributes a number of installations too including a complete drystone cottage and a clay tree while Sam Durant's "Scaffold", a protest interpretation of a gallows, has an unlikely secondary function as a children's climbing frame.

Edinburgh International Climbing Arena (EICA)

MAP P.122
South Platt Hill, Ratho. ☎ 0131 333 6333, Ⓦ edinburghleisure.co.uk. Mon–Fri 8am–10pm, Sat & Sun 9am–6pm. Adult climb £10.80. Child Clip 'n Climb £9. Take a tram westbound to Edinburgh Park and change onto bus #20 westbound. Alight at

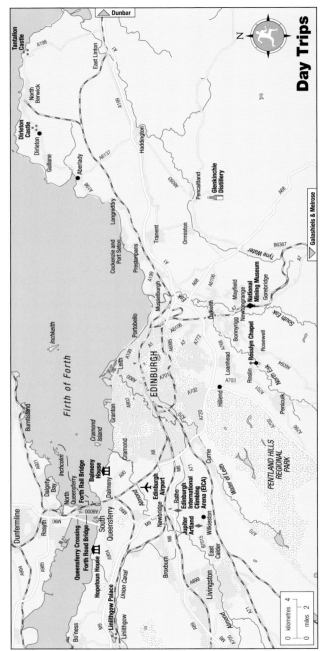

Day Trips

Ratho and walk for two minutes west along the canal. By car, follow signs from the A8 westbound

Europe's largest indoor climbing centre, the **Edinburgh International Climbing Arena (EICA)** is built into the remnants of a disused quarry on the banks of the Union Canal. The place is truly gigantic and some of the climbs here challenge not only your skills and stamina but also your head for heights. You'll need to bring a partner to belay with, and ideally that person will have completed a short belaying course. If you don't have your own harness, any necessary equipment can be bought or hired from the shop within the complex. For the kids' Clip 'n Climb the course belaying is automated. There are also a number of rope-free boulders here on which you can practise specific techniques with a crash mat below to break your fall.

Dalmeny House

MAP P.122

Dalmeny Estate, 3 miles east of Queensferry ☏ 0131 331 1888, ⊛ dalmeny.co.uk. June & July only, Sun–Wed guided tours at 2.15pm & 3.30pm, £10. On foot, follow Queensferry High Street eastwards for 1.5 miles until you reach the estate entrance. By car, follow signposts from the A90 near Queensferry.

Set on a two-thousand-acre estate between South Queensferry and Cramond, this Tudor revivalist manor may not be the prettiest country seat you'll encounter in Scotland, but the quality of the items on show at **Dalmeny House** make it a fascinating place to visit. As well as some of the finest baroque and Neoclassical furniture produced for Louis' XIV, XV and XVI in the hundred years before the French Revolution, there's also a valuable selection of memorabilia relating to Napoleon Bonaparte. The art collection is surprisingly strong too with a very rare set of tapestries made from cartoons by Goya, and portraits by Raeburn, Reynolds, Gainsborough and Lawrence.

Hopetoun House

MAP P.122

Hopetoun Estate, 3 miles west of Queensferry ☏ 0131 331 2451, ⊛ hopetoun. co.uk. Easter–Sept daily 10.30am–5pm. £9.85 house and grounds, £4.55 grounds only. Free tour daily at 2pm. On foot, follow the coastline westwards from Queensferry for 3 miles; by car, take M90 turn off onto the A904 and follow signs.

Sitting in its own extensive estate on the south shore of the Forth, **Hopetoun House** is one of the most impressive stately homes in Scotland. The original house was built at the turn of the eighteenth century for the first earl of Hopetoun by Sir William Bruce, the architect of Holyroodhouse. A couple of decades later, William Adam carried out an enormous extension, engulfing the structure with a curvaceous main facade and two projecting wings – superb examples of Roman Baroque pomp and swagger. Hopetoun's architecture is undoubtedly its most compelling feature, but the furnishings aren't completely overwhelmed, with some impressive seventeenth-century tapestries, Meissen porcelain

Hopetoun House

and a distinguished collection of paintings, including portraits by Gainsborough, Ramsay and Raeburn. The house's grounds include a long, regal driveway and lovely walks along woodland trails and the banks of the Forth.

Inchcolm Island

MAP P.122

Five miles northeast of South Queensferry near the Fife shore. From South Queensferry: Maid of the Forth, Hawes Pier ☎ 0131 331 5000, ⓦ maidoftheforth.co.uk. April–Oct times vary, more regular in high season. Check websites for timetables. £20 for 1hr 30min landing trip. From Edinburgh's Waverley Bridge: Forth Boat Tours ☎ 0870 118 1866, ⓦ forthtours.com. 2–5 landing trips lasting 1hr 30min daily between Easter & Oct, some weekend sailings also in winter. £26 including bus from Edinburgh. Home to the best-preserved medieval abbey in Scotland, **Inchcolm Island** was founded in 1235 after King Alexander I was stormbound here and took refuge in a hermit's cell. Although the structure as a whole is half-ruined today, the tower, octagonal chapterhouse and echoing cloisters are intact and well worth exploring. The hour and a half you're given ashore by the boat timetables also allows time for a picnic on the abbey's lawns or the chance to explore Inchcolm's old military fortifications and extensive bird-nesting grounds.

Linlithgow Palace

MAP P.122

Kirkgate, Linlithgow, just off the M9 motorway. By train: 4 hourly; 20min. ☎ 01506 842 896. Daily: April–Sept 9.30am–5.30pm; Oct–March 10am–4.30pm; HES. £6. **Linlithgow Palace** is a splendid fifteenth-century ruin, romantically set on the edge of Linlithgow Loch and associated with some of Scotland's best-known historical figures, including Mary, Queen of Scots, who was born here on December 8, 1542 and became queen six days later. A royal manor house is believed to have existed on this site since the time of David I, though James I began construction of the present palace, a process that continued through two centuries and the reign of no fewer than eight monarchs. From the top of the northwest tower, Queen Margaret looked out in vain for the return of James IV from the field of Flodden in 1513 – indeed, the views from her bower, six storeys up from the ground, are

Linlithgow Palace

exceptional. The ornate octagonal fountain in the inner courtyard, with its wonderfully intricate figures and medallion heads, flowed with wine for the wedding of James V and Mary of Guise.

Rosslyn Chapel

MAP P.122

Chapel Loan, Roslin, 7 miles south of Edinburgh just off the A701 ☏ 0131 440 2159, ⓦ rosslynchapel.com. Sept–May Mon–Sat 9.30am–5pm, Sun noon–4.45pm; June–Aug Mon–Sat 9.30am–6pm, Sun noon–4.45pm. £9. Bus #15 westbound from Princes Street in Edinburgh.

As much revered for its sublime stone carvings – some of the finest in the world – as its alleged crusader connections, **Rosslyn Chapel** is more cathedral-like in its dimensions. It was intended to be a huge collegiate church dedicated to St Matthew, but construction halted soon after the founder's death in 1484, and the vestry built onto the facade nearly four hundred years later is the sole subsequent addition. After a long period of neglect, a massive fifteen-year restoration project has recently been completed.

Rosslyn's exterior bristles with pinnacles, gargoyles, flying buttresses and canopies, while inside the **stonework** is, if anything, even more intricate. The foliage carving is particularly outstanding, with botanically accurate depictions of over a dozen different leaves and plants. Among them are cacti and Indian corn, compounding the legend that the founder's grandfather, the daring sea adventurer Prince Henry of Orkney, did indeed set foot in the New World a century before Columbus. The rich and subtle figurative sculptures have given Rosslyn the nickname of "a bible in stone", though they're more allegorical than literal, with portrayals of the Dance of Death, the Seven Acts of Mercy and the Seven Deadly Sins.

Rosslyn Chapel

National Mining Museum

MAP P.122

8 miles southeast of Edinburgh on the A7, Lady Victoria Colliery, Newtongrange ☏ 0131 663 7519, ⓦ nationalminingmuseum.com. Tours range from £4.50 to £9. Trains run from Edinburgh Waverley to Newtongrange every 30min (22min); by bus, #29 & #33 from Princes Street southbound.

Closed in 1989 this Victorian colliery, now the **National Mining Museum**, is one of the best preserved in the world. A variety of exhibits show numerous engineering innovations throughout the years, including the largest steam engine in Scotland, originally used to haul men up and down the pit shaft. The site is truly vast and much of the colliery will remain in the renovation queue for years to come, giving the place an atmospheric ambiance of decay. Ex-minor tour guides offer real insight into what it was like to work here while you absorb the sights, smells and sounds of the working pit.

Pentland Hills

MAP P.122

Buses #4 and #15 westbound from Princes Street will take you to Hillend at the foot of the hills.

The Pentland Hills

The **Pentland Hills**, a chain some eighteen miles long and five wide, dominate most views south of Edinburgh and offer walkers and mountain bikers a thrilling taste of wild Scottish countryside just beyond the suburbs.

The simplest way to get a taste of the scenery of the Pentlands is to set off from the car park by the ski centre at **Hillend**, at the northeast end of the range; take the path up the right-hand side of the dry ski slopes, turning left shortly after crossing a stile to reach a prominent point with outstanding views over Edinburgh and Fife.

Glenkinchie Distillery

MAP P.122

7 miles southwest of Haddinton on the A6093, turn south at Pencaitland onto Lempockwells Road and follow the signs for two miles ☎ 01875 342 012 ⓦ malts. com. Nov–Feb daily 10am–4pm, March–Oct daily 10am–5pm, last tour 1hr before closing. £10–14; 1hr 15min.

The **Glenkinchie Distillery** is the closest place to Edinburgh where the uisce beatha – the water of life – is produced. Here, of course, they emphasize the qualities that set Glenkinchie, a lighter, drier malt, apart from the peaty, smoky

whiskies of the north and west. On display, there's a pleasant little exhibition featuring some quaint distilling relics, which enhance the factory tour experience almost as much as the free dram finale.

Melrose and its Abbey

MAP P.122

37 miles southeast of Edinburgh ☎ 0131 668 8081. Daily: April–Sept 9.30am–5.30pm; Oct–March 10am–4pm. HES £6. By car, follow the A7 south to Galashiels then take A6091. By train, Edinburgh to Tweedbank every 30mins; 55min. Take a taxi or bus link for the last two miles to Melrose.

Tucked in between the River Tweed and the gorse-backed Eildon Hills, minuscule **Melrose** is one of the most appealing towns in the Borders. Centred on its busy little market square, its narrow streets are trimmed by a harmonious ensemble of styles, from pretty little cottages and tweedy shops to high-standing Georgian and Victorian facades.

Its chief draw is the twelfth-century pink- and red-tinted stone ruins of **Melrose Abbey** that soar above their riverside surroundings.

Legend has it that the heart of Robert I is buried at Melrose Abbey (his body having been buried at Dunfermline Abbey), and in 1997, when a heart cask was publicly exhumed, this theory received an unexpected boost.

North Berwick

MAP P.122

24 miles east of Edinburgh. By car, follow the A1 from Edinburgh until the junction for A198. Trains run hourly from Waverley Station (33min). Boat trips to Bass Rock from the Scottish Seabird Centre: Harbour Lodge, 7 Beach Road ☎ 01620 890 202, ⓦ seabird.org, April–Oct, daily: times vary. Price ranges from £20–£130 depending on itinerary.

North Berwick has a great deal of charm and a somewhat faded, old-fashioned air, its guesthouses and hotels extending along the shore in all their Victorian and Edwardian sobriety. The town's small harbour is set on a headland which cleaves two crescents of golden sand, providing the town with an attractive coastal setting. A short distance offshore the Bass Rock rises vertiginously from the sea and gives the town its defining characteristic. Described by David Attenborough as "one of the twelve wonders of the world", the small island is home to one hundred and fifty thousand gannets that thrill boat trippers with their diving raids on the choppy waters below.

Tantallon Castle

MAP P.122

3 miles east of North Berwick on the A198 ☎ 01620 892 727. April–Sept daily 9.30am–5.30pm; Oct–March daily 10am–4pm. HES. £6. From North Berwick take the Dunbar bus (Eves Coaches #120; Mon–Sat 6 daily, 2 on Sun; 6 mins); on foot, you can walk there from town along the cliffs in around an hour.

The melodramatic ruins of the fourteenth-century **Tantallon Castle** stand on the precipitous cliffs facing the Bass Rock. With a sheer drop down to the sea on three sides and a sequence of moats and ditches on the fourth, the castle's desolate invincibility is daunting, especially when the wind howls over the remaining battlements and the surf crashes on the rocks far below.

Dirleton Castle

MAP P.122

2.5 miles west of North Berwick signposted off the A198 ☎ 01620 850 330. April–Sept daily 9.30am–5.30pm; otherwise daily 9.30am–4.30pm. HES. £6. First Bus #124 from the High Street in North Berwick (Mon–Sun every half hour; 15min).

The genteel hamlet of **Dirleton** huddles around its romantic thirteenth-century ruin that saw action in the Wars of Scottish Independence. It was later rendered militarily defunct after a besiegement by Oliver Cromwell's army to flush out bandits. Today it's an attractive relic, largely intact, with restored Victorian gardens making for a popular wedding venue.

Dunbar

MAP P.122

30 miles east of Edinburgh. By train every 30 to 60min; 25min. By car, follow the A1 east from Edinburgh. John Muir Birthplace: 126 High Street ☎ 01368 865 899, ⓦ jmbt. org.uk. April–Sept Mon–Sat 10am–5pm, Sun 1–5pm; Oct–March same times but closed Mon & Tues. Free.

The coastal town of **Dunbar** with its delightfully intricate double harbour set beside the shattered remains of a once-mighty castle is today best known globally as the birthplace of nineteenth-century explorer and naturalist, John Muir (1838–1914), who created the United States' national park system. Muir spent his formative years here growing up in one of grand old stone buildings, now a free museum, that grace the recently spruced-up High Street.

While Muir might have left for America, the remaining townspeople were left to make a living from the choppy North Sea and while today's inhabitants are more likely to be city bound commuters than fisher-folk, the town's new-found destination as a surfing hotspot is keeping the place ticking over.

Dunbar harbour

ACCOMMODATION

The Old Rectory Suite at The Witchery Apartments

Accommodation

Already a tourism hotspot, Edinburgh's recent upsurge in visitor numbers has seen the number of hotels and aparthotels in the city grow exponentially. This, together with Airbnb's seemingly irrepressible march, has resulted in a bewildering choice of places to stay in the city. Bargains are always there to be found, usually by way of a last-minute booking or via a promotions agency and if you're on a really tight budget, there are plenty of hostels particularly around the Old Town. Making reservations is worthwhile at any time of year, and is strongly recommended for stays during the Festival and around Hogmanay when prices swell considerably and spaces get booked months in advance.

Old Town

APEX GRASSMARKET Map p.48. Pocket map B16. 31–35 Grassmarket ☎ 0131 300 3456, Ⓦ apexhotels.co.uk. £145. This ex-university building turned 175-bed business-oriented hotel has comfortable rooms, some with unencumbered views to the Castle and balconies that peer down onto Grassmarket below. Up top there's a double-rosette rooftop restaurant with a dramatic skyline view – especially after dark – while downstairs you'll find a small pool and gym.

GREYFRIARS APARTMENTS Map p.48. Pocket map C15. Around the Royal Mile ☎ 07794 875 890, Ⓦ greyfriars-apartments. com. A one-bed apartment for two people is around £125. Among the best value in town, the six moderately spacious apartments offered by Greyfriars are stylishly presented and superbly located; all are just off the Royal Mile or nearby. You'll need to book early, especially if you're planning a weekend trip.

IBIS EDINBURGH CENTRE Map p.48. Pocket map D15. 6 Hunter Square ☎ 0131 619 2800, Ⓦ ibis.com. £125. Probably the best-located chain hotel cheapie in the Old Town, within sight of the Royal Mile; rooms are modern and inexpensive, but there are few facilities other than a rather plain bar.

MOTEL ONE – EDINBURGH ROYAL Map p.48. Pocket map C15. 18–21 Market St ☎ 0131 220 0730, Ⓦ motel-one.com. £104. Located between the Old and New Towns and across from the station, this modern hotel cheapie is an ideal base for exploring the city. The best rooms have views onto Princes Street Gardens, as does the hotel's spacious bar.

TRAVELODGE EDINBURGH CENTRAL Map p.48. Pocket map E15. 33 St Mary's St ☎ 0871 984 6137, Ⓦ travelodge.co.uk. £91. There's more than a hint of concrete brutalism in the look of this chain hotel, but it's well priced and centrally located, 100 yards from the Royal Mile near some excellent restaurants. At weekends it tends to fill up with stag and hen parties but the rooms are quiet enough if a little grungy.

THE WITCHERY APARTMENTS Map p.48. Pocket map B15. Castlehill ☎ 0131 225 5613, Ⓦ thewitchery.com. £365. Nine riotously indulgent suites grouped around this famously spooky restaurant just downhill from the castle; expect antique furniture, big leather armchairs, tapestry-draped beds, oak panelling and huge roll-top baths, as well as ultramodern sound systems and complimentary champagne.

Southside

94DR Map p.30. Pocket map G7. 94 Dalkeith Rd ☎ 0131 662 9265, Ⓦ 94dr.

com. £130. A boutique guesthouse offering three different styles with its couture, bespoke and tailored rooms. Front-facing ones have a view of Arthur's Seat.

TEN HILL PLACE Map p.30. Pocket map E16. 10 Hill Place ☎ 0131 662 2080, ⓦ tenhillplace.com. £170. A contemporary, efficient hotel linked to the historic Royal College of Surgeons, with 78 sleek and smartly styled bedrooms, all run according to an environmentally conscious policy.

UNIVERSITY OF EDINBURGH POLLOCK HALLS OF RESIDENCE Map p.30. Pocket map G7. 18 Holyrood Park Rd ☎ 0131 651 2007, ⓦ edinburghfirst.com. Singles £48; doubles £112.50; flats £525/week. Unquestionably the best setting of any of the city's university accommodation, right beside Holyrood Park, just southeast of the Old Town. It provides single rooms, doubles and self-catering flats, mostly available Easter & June to mid-Sept, though some rooms are available year-round.

New Town

ARDENLEE GUEST HOUSE Map p.78. Pocket map D2. 9 Eyre Place ☎ 0131 556 2838, ⓦ ardenleeguesthouse.com. £120. Welcoming guesthouse at the foot of the New Town, with original Victorian features and nine reasonably spacious rooms, seven of which are en suite and some suitable for families. A two-bed Georgian apartment (£150) is also available, close by at 3 Eyre Place.

EDEN LOCKE Map p.78. Pocket map C4. 127 George St ☎ 0131 526 4190, ⓦ lockeliving.com. £150. Hotels for hipsters; Eden Locke offers on-trend Gryzwinski and Pons designed apart-hotel studios with corner sofas and curated artworks. The kitchens are small but somehow fit in a washer-dryer and dishwasher, while the bathroom comes with apothecary skin products and a rubber duck.

GERALD'S PLACE Map p.78. Pocket map D3. 21b Abercromby Place ☎ 0131 558 7017, ⓦ geraldsplace.com. £120. A homely taste of New Town life at an upmarket but hospitable and comfy basement B&B. The

rustic decor is tasteful, with some fine artwork and old books to catch your eye, while the breakfasts are generous, with many homemade components.

THE GUEST ROOM Map p.78. Pocket map D3. 31a Nelson St ☎ 0131 556 4798, ⓦ theguestroom.co.uk. £115. A notably unobtrusive B&B offering two spacious rooms with a choice of courtyard or garden views. Start the day with a breakfast tray of berries, porridge and freshly squeezed orange.

HOLIDAY INN EXPRESS EDINBURGH CITY CENTRE Map p.78. Pocket map E3. Picardy Place ☎ 0131 558 2300, ⓦ ihg.com. £148. It's by a busy roundabout, but otherwise in a good location in an elegant old Georgian tenement near the top of Broughton St, with 161 rooms featuring neat but predictable chain-hotel decor and facilities.

THE GLASSHOUSE Map p.78. Pocket map F3. 2 Greenside Place ☎ 0131 525 8200, ⓦ theglasshousehotel.co.uk. £250. Incorporating the castellated facade of the former Lady Glenorchy's Church, this ultra-hip hotel has 65 chichi rooms with push-button curtains and sliding doors opening onto a huge, lush roof garden scattered with Philippe Starck furniture. Perfect if you're in town for a weekend of indulgence.

PRINCIPLE EDINBURGH Map p.78. Pocket map B13. 19–21 George St ☎ 0131 225 1251, ⓦ phcompany.com/ principle/edinburgh-george-street. £220. A beautiful example of a prime Georgian building, inside and out, thanks to its Neoclassical frontage and sympathetically harmonious decor. The suites are luxurious from top to tail and often come with lofty views north to the Firth of Forth.

NIRA CALEDONIA Map p.78. Pocket map C3. 6 Gloucester Place ☎ 0131 225 2720, ⓦ niracaledonia.com. £150. Elegant and comfortable townhouse hotel located on a typical New Town terrace. Decor is modern, opulent and striking, if a little overwhelming.

RABBLE Map p.78. Pocket map A13. 55a Frederick St ☎ 0131 622 7800, ⓦ rabbleedinburgh.co.uk. £180. Ten much-sought-after rooms at the back of the popular New Town bar and restaurant. Beautifully styled with beds fitted with walnut headboards and plush fabrics, they look out onto a cobbled lane behind.

REGENT HOUSE Map p.78. Pocket map E3. 3 Forth St, Broughton ☎ 0131 556 1616, ⓦ regenthousehotel.co.uk. £90. A good value small hotel over four floors that makes up for its lack of glamour with a great location, right in the heart of Broughton on a quiet side street. Some rooms are big enough to accommodate three to five people.

ROCK HOUSE Map p.78. Pocket map D13. 28 Calton Hill ☎ 0131 558 1108, ⓦ rockhouse-edinburgh.com. From £560 to £950 per week for the 2 person studio, £700 to £1300 for the four person apartment, £1400 to £2950 for the main house. A trio of exquisite holiday let properties just one minute's walk from Princes Street, yet in an improbable village-like setting on Calton Hill's western incline. Rock House was built in the 1750s; a delightful orange lime-wash frontage surrounding a formal water garden with a converted octagonal photographer's studio to the side. The two buildings – divided into three units, with log fires, William Morris paper and muddy green sofas – balance taste and luxury to perfection.

TIGERLILY Map p.78. Pocket map C4. 125 George St ☎ 0131 225 5005, ⓦ tigerlilyedinburgh.co.uk. £225. A glitzy boutique hotel, bar and restaurant that epitomizes the excess of 21st-century George Street. A classic Georgian townhouse transformed into a flamboyant design extravaganza; indulgent pink or black bedroom suites are kitted out with decadent fabrics and some even have a real fire.

Leith and North Edinburgh

MALMAISON Map p.100. Pocket map C11. 1 Tower Place ☎ 0131 285 1478, ⓦ malmaison.com. £105. Chic, modern hotel set in the grand old seamen's hostel just back from the wharf-side. Bright, bold original designs in each room, plus a gym, room service, Parisian brasserie and café-bar serving lighter meals.

MILLARS 64 Map p.100. Pocket map F2. 64 Pilrig St ☎ 0131 454 3666, ⓦ millars64.com. £90. The archetypal B&B striving for perfection in every way. Spotlessly clean from top to bottom, beautifully cooked breakfasts and homemade shortbread on the hospitality tray. A combination that saw them win Best B&B in the UK at to the 2017 Food and Travel Reader awards.

Hostels

ARGYLE BACKPACKERS Map p.116. Pocket map E7. 14 Argyle Place, Marchmont ☎ 0131 667 9991, ⓦ argyle-backpackers.com. A quiet, less intense version of the typical backpackers' hostel, pleasantly located in several adjoining townhouses near the Meadows park in studenty Marchmont, just south of the Old Town. The dorms are small – up to 6 beds per room – and there are a dozen or so twin rooms as well as a communal conservatory and garden at the back.

CASTLE ROCK HOSTEL Map p.30. Pocket map B16. 15 Johnston Terrace, ☎ 0131 225 9666, ⓦ castlerockedinburgh.com. Dorm £11; double £45. Tucked below the Castle

ramparts, with two hundred or so beds arranged in large, bright dorms, as well as triple and quads and some doubles. The communal areas include a games room with pool and table tennis plus a sunny patio.

EDINBURGH CENTRAL SYHA Map p.100. Pocket map F3. 9 Haddington Place ☎ 0131 524 2090, ⓦ syha.org.uk. Private rooms £64; dorms £15. In a handy location at the top of Leith Walk (a five minute stroll from the centre), this five-star hostel has single, double and triple private rooms as well as eight-bed dorms with en-suite facilities. There is a reasonably priced bistro in addition to self-catering kitchen facilities.

HIGH STREET HOSTEL Map p.30. Pocket map D15. 8 Blackfriars St ☎ 0131 557 3984, ⓦ highstreethostel.com. Twin rooms £54; dorms £10–14 depending on size. Lively and popular hostel in an attractive sixteenth-century building just off the Royal Mile with dorms of up to 18 beds and twin rooms. The communal facilities include a kitchen, a quiet room and a large party dining lounge with piano and pool table.

KICK ASS HOSTELS Map p.48. Pocket map B16. 2 West Port ☎ 0131 226 6351, ⓦ kickasshostels.co.uk. Dorms range from £7 to £28 depending on size and season. With its own in-house café and pub, and segregated dorms some of which have a clear view up to the castle, this is a year-round popular stop attracting a young crowd. The rooms sleep up to 12 and have USB power points, lockers and electronic swipe cards.

SAFESTAY EDINBURGH Map p.30. Pocket map D15. 50 Blackfriars St ☎ 0131 524 1989, ⓦ smartcityhostels.com. Private twin £85; dorms £28. An upmarket hostel just off the Royal Mile, with twin rooms or dorms accommodating up to twelve guests. The café serves good-value food and breakfasts, and there is a late-night bar exclusively for residents plus a little courtyard with tables.

STAY CENTRAL HOTEL Map p.48. Pocket map C15. 139 Cowgate ☎ 0131 622 6801, ⓦ staycentral.co.uk. Doubles £126; party dorms for 6 £320. A popular option for large stag and hen groups, this neoteric hotel has lots of rooms that sleep up to six including the 'Ultimate Party Room" with table tennis, a dart board and a big fridge. If you're partying hard, the hotel can arrange for a booze delivery and a live DJ set in your room.

Campsites

DRUMMOHR CARAVAN AND CAMPING PARK Levenhall, Musselburgh, on the B1348 ☎ 0131 665 6867, ⓦ drummohr. org. Bothies 2-4 people £60; lodges £160; camping per pitch £22. A large, pleasant site on the eastern edge of Musselburgh, a coastal satellite town to the east of Edinburgh, with excellent transport connections to the city centre. As well as the usual pitches, there are a few "bothies" (basic wooden huts that sleep

four) and the more luxurious lodges that sleep eight.

EDINBURGH CARAVAN CLUB Site 35 Marine Drive, Silverknowes, 5 miles northwest of the centre ☎ 0131 312 6874, ⓦ caravanclub.co.uk £15/pitch. Caravan-dominated site in a pleasant location close to the shoreline, though there's little else here. Cramond village is a ten-minute walk west along the shore and has a pub and cafés.

ESSENTIALS

Princes Street

Arrival

The quickest, easiest and cheapest way to get to Edinburgh is by plane, either via Edinburgh Airport or Glasgow Airport, which handles most transatlantic and long-haul flights. Edinburgh's train, tram and bus terminals are within walking distance of each other in the heart of the city.

By plane

Travel from Edinburgh **airport** to the city centre is fast and economical, while Glasgow is very well connected to Edinburgh by train and bus.

Edinburgh

Edinburgh Airport (☏ 0844 448 8833, ⓦ edinburghairport.com) lies around six miles west of the city centre, just off the M8 and M9 motorways. The cheapest way into town is by **bus**, most conveniently on the Airlink #100 (24hr; journey 20–45min), departing from just outside Domestic Arrivals (Stance D), and terminating at Waverley Bridge, just outside Edinburgh Waverley train station (see page 137). Services run every 10min between 4.30am and 12.35am the following day, and every 30min through the night, with tickets priced at £4.50 single and £7.50 open return. If you're staying in Leith you might want to take the Skylink #200 service (changes to #N22 through the night; Stance D), departing from Stance B and with timetable and ticket prices broadly similar, though the journey can take almost an hour at peak times. Tickets for both Airlink and Sylink service can be bought at the kiosk outside Domestic Arrivals, though it's easier to pay in cash on board and – unlike most city buses – change is given. Cheapest and most circuitous of all the airport bus services is the regular Lothian Bus #35 (roughly every 10–30min, 5.56am–11.05pm; journey 45min–1hr 15min), which departs from Stance F, stops on the Royal Mile and also terminates in Leith. Single fares are £1.60 (no change given, so you'll need the exact fare), though a day pass (£4) can be great value if you arrive in the morning and plan on a busy day's sightseeing. For detailed route and timetable info on all services see ⓦ lothianbuses. co.uk/airport. If you fancy travelling in a little more style, the new **tram** service (ⓦ edinburghtrams.com) runs from the airport to Princes Street (daily 6.18am–10.48pm, every 7–10min; journey 31min) and costs £5.50 single, £8.50 return. Tickets are available from the machines on the platform. You can also buy tickets for the tram and all airport bus services via the Transport for Edinburgh mobile app (see page 138). Both metered **taxis** and fixed-price private hire from the airport to the city centre cost upwards of £20, with a journey time of around 20min depending on traffic. Capital Cars (☏ 0131 777 7777, ⓦ capitalcarsscotland.co.uk) offer a meet-and-greet service for an additional £12.

Glasgow

Glasgow Airport (☏ 0844 481 5555, ⓦ glasgowairport.com) lies around eight miles west of Glasgow city centre, near Paisley. The 24hr Glasgow Airport Express #500 **bus** service (every 10min; journey 25min), is the fastest option for onward transport to the city centre, departing from Stance 1, stopping at Queen Street train station (for onward train travel to Edinburgh) and terminating at Buchanan Street bus station (for onward coach travel to Edinburgh). Tickets are priced at £7.50 single and £10 open return. Though there's no rail link with the centre at present, plans were recently announced for a possible tram-train service with a journey time of 15min, and construction envisaged to begin in 2021. Taxis cost upwards of £20 to the city centre, depending on traffic. In terms of journey time and frequency, there's not much to choose between bus and train when thinking about **onward travel** to Edinburgh; both depart every 10–15min during the day and take around 1hr 10–20min. Citylink (☎ 0871 266 3333, ⓦ citylink. co.uk) is the main coach operator, with tickets priced at £7.60 single, £11.60 open return; services run half-hourly from 7.30pm till midnight and then hourly till 5am, with all buses from 11am till 4am serving the airport. Trains (ⓦ scotrail.co.uk) are significantly more expensive at £12.60 off-peak single (£13.90 peak); there are no open returns. If you're travelling at peak times, note that – being the busiest commuter route in Scotland – services can get very crowded, often with standing room only.

By train and coach

Arriving by train from elsewhere in Britain (or the south of Scotland), your service will terminate in Edinburgh Waverley (☎ 0345 748 4950, ⓦ networkrail.co.uk/stations/ edinburgh-waverley/) at the east end of Princes Street, served by most city bus routes. If arriving from Glasgow or the north, your service will first make a stop at the city's other main station, Haymarket, useful if you're staying in the West End. Travelling by **bus** or **coach** from elsewhere in either Britain (☎ 08717 818178, ⓦ nationalexpress.com) or Scotland (☎ 0871 266 3333, ⓦ citylink.co.uk), you'll arrive in the terminal on St Andrew Square, at the east end of Princes Street, a 2min walk from Waverley and a 1min walk from the tram terminus on York Place.

Getting around

Although Edinburgh occupies a large area relative to its population (just over half a million people), most places worth visiting lie within the compact city centre, which is easily explored on foot or by bike. There's nevertheless a generally efficient – if often congested – **public transport network**, consisting for the most part of buses, with most services terminating on, or passing through or near, Princes Street, the city's main thoroughfare. Though it's unlikely you'll need it for most journeys, the bus station is located just north of here off the corner of St Andrew Square.

Tramspotting

Almost as infamous as Irvine Welsh's novel, and doubtless having clocked up even more column inches, Edinburgh's hugely controversial **tram project** finally reached completion in spring 2014 after almost six highly fraught years. At long last, Edinburgh Airport had a **modern rail link** to the city centre. The end product may have been two and a half lines short, suffered a chaotic construction which tested the good citizens of Edinburgh's patience to breaking point, coming in over double its initial budget, but the solitary 14km of line which finally emerged has confounded critics by turning a profit two years ahead of schedule and exceeding passenger targets. In late 2015, after yet more discussion and delay, Edinburgh Council finally gave the green light to extend the line to Newhaven, just beyond Leith's Ocean Terminal, as originally planned.

Transport for Edinburgh app

The free **Transport for Edinburgh mobile app** (Ⓦlothianbuses.co.uk/apps) allows you to buy bundles of electronic tickets for both bus and tram, particularly useful if you'll be making single bus trips on various days, but not enough to justify a Ridacard (see below) – minimum spend is £10, and you'll also be able to access live departure info for every bus route in the city.

Buses

The city is fairly well served by buses; by far the largest majority of these are the iconic maroon double-deckers operated by **Lothian Buses** (Ⓣ0131 555 6363, Ⓦlothianbuses.co.uk), and all services referred to in the guide are run by Lothian unless otherwise stated. All services are numbered and most run at a daytime frequency of 10–20min. A reduced network of **night buses** also operates, with departures every hour or so (every 10min on some services at weekends) and with their route numbers prefixed by 'N'. Every bus stop displays maps indicating which services frequent it and the routes they take; an increasing number also have live departure information. Single **fares** are priced at £1.60 (£3 for night buses) and the easiest way to pay is in cash as you board, though no change is issued so you'll need the exact coinage. Other options include a day ticket (£4) allowing unlimited travel on bus or tram (again, paying for this in cash as you board is easiest), and a Ridacard pass (£18), allowing a week's unlimited travel on bus (including night services) and tram. Ridacards and indeed any tickets can be bought from the Lothian Bus Travelshops at 31 Waverley Bridge (Mon & Thurs 9am–7pm, Tues, Wed & Fri 9am–6pm, Sat 9am–5.30pm); 9 Clifton Terrace (Mon–Fri 8am–6pm, Sat 9am–5.30pm); or 27 Hanover St (Mon–Fri 9am–6pm, Sat 9am–5.30pm). If you don't fancy fiddling with coins every time you travel, you might

also want to download the Transport for Edinburgh app (see box). For an excellent map of the entire network see Ⓦlothianbuses.co.uk.

The predominantly white, single-decker buses of First Edinburgh (Ⓣ01224 650 100, Ⓦfirstgroup.com) run services on a number of the main routes through the city, but are better for outlying towns and villages. They have their own system of tickets and day tickets, similar in structure to Lothian Buses, though drivers will always give change. Most services depart from or near the main bus station at St Andrew Square.

Trams

While you may well use Edinburgh's solitary **tram line** (Ⓦedinburghtrams.com) to get to and from the airport, it's fairly unlikely you'll use it for much else, serving as it does largely suburban and commuter destinations in the city's far west. The terminal is on York Place in the New Town, just behind the bus station. Services depart every 7min daily from 5.30am to 11.30pm, with a single ticket (excluding the airport) costing £1.60; Lothian Buses day passes (see page 138) and Ridacards (see page 138) are also valid. Tram tickets must be purchased from the ticket machines prior to boarding; credit and debit cards accepted.

Cycling

Although hilly, Edinburgh is a reasonably bike-friendly city, with a growing network of **cycle paths**, particularly in the university areas south of the centre. Local cycling advocacy group Spokes publishes an excellent map of the city with recommended cycle routes; pick up a copy at the tourist office. Bicycle rental is available from Biketrax, 11–13 Lochrin Place, Tolcross (£17/day then £13 for additional days; ☎0131 228 6633, ⓦbiketrax.co.uk), and Edinburgh Cycle Hire, 29 Blackfriars St (from £25/day; ☎0131 556 5560, ⓦcyclescotland.co.uk). The latter also offers scenic guided city **cycle tours** (£35/person; electric bike option available for same price) taking in the likes of Holyrood Park, Arthur's Seat, the *Sheep Heid Inn* (see page 65) and Dr Neil's Garden (see page 63).

Taxis
Edinburgh is well endowed with **taxi ranks**, and you can also hail black cabs on the street. All taxis are metered and costs are reasonable – from the city centre to Leith, for example, costs around £9. Companies include Central Taxis (☎0131 229 2468, ⓦtaxis-edinburgh.co.uk) and City Cabs (☎0131 228 1211, ⓦcitycabs.co.uk). Uber (ⓦuber.com) users will have little trouble finding a ride as the city is comprehensively covered.

Sightseeing tours and guided walks
Year round, a fleet of state-of-the-art **open-top double-deckers** run by Edinburgh Bus Tours (☎0131 556 2244, ⓦedinburghtour.com; daily roughly 9am–6pm; every 10–15min; 1hr; £15) line up on Waverley Bridge, hoovering up the tourists pouring out of Waverley Station and the Airlink bus (see page 136). Several themed tours are available covering most of the major sights, as well as a summer option to South Queensferry (see page 120) combined with a

cruise on the Firth of Forth (3hr; £35). Unsurprisingly for such an atmospheric city, Edinburgh is served by countless **walking** tours. As well as traditional historical tours (for which the family-run Edinburgh Guided Tour has one of the best reputations: ☎07927 904695, ⓦedinburghguidedtour.com), there are myriad – and often highly acclaimed – specialist variations covering almost every conceivable theme from the inevitable ghosts to Harry Potter (☎07977 934274, ⓦedinburghwalkingtour.co.uk/harry-potter-walk.html), gourmet food and drink (☎07740 869359, ⓦeatwalkedinburgh.co.uk), small-group photography (☎07795 337778, ⓦjameschristiephotography.com), Inspector Rebus (ⓦrebustours.com) and of course, Outlander (☎0131 225 5445, ⓦmercattours.com). Tours last anything from an hour or two to a whole day, and while many are priced in the £10–30 range, some of the specialist ones can cost double that. If you're on a budget, opt for one of the numerous cheap and cheerful free tours (ⓦedinburghfreetour.com, ⓦneweuropetours.eu/edinburgh).

Directory A-Z

Addresses
Edinburgh addresses come with postcodes at the end, consisting of the letters EH and a number giving the geographical location of the street in relation to the city. A further number and two letters specifies its location more precisely. Note that these numbers don't correspond to the actual distance from the centre.

Costs
Edinburgh is by far the most **expensive** city in Scotland, and, according to a recent survey, tops

London as the most expensive short break destination in the UK. A plunging pound in the wake of the Brexit vote has nevertheless eased costs for foreign visitors at least. The minimum expenditure for a couple staying at hostels, self-catering and eating the odd meal out is around £55–60 each per day. Staying at budget B&Bs, eating at unpretentious restaurants and visiting the odd tourist attraction, means spending at least £75 each per day. If you're renting a car, staying in comfortable B&Bs or hotels and eating well, you should reckon on at least £100 a day per person.

Crime

Edinburgh is a generally safe city, though should you have anything stolen or be involved in an incident that requires reporting, dial ☏ 101 from any location; ☏ 999 should only be used in emergencies – in other words if someone is in immediate danger or a crime is taking place.

Electricity

Electricity supply in Edinburgh conforms to the EU standard of approximately 230V. Sockets are designed for British **three-pin plugs**, which are different from those in Europe and North America.

Embassies and consulates

Consulate General of Ireland, 16 Randolph Crescent (☏ 0131 226 7711, ⓦ dfa.ie/irish-consulate/edinburgh/); US Consulate, 3 Regent Terrace (☏ 0131 556 8315, ⓦ uk.usembassy. gov/embassy-consulates/edinburgh).

Football

While the rivalry between Edinburgh's two footballing giants **Hearts** (☏ 0333 043 1874, ⓦ heartsfc.co.uk) and **Hibernian** (☏ 0844 844 1875, ⓦ hibernianfc.co.uk), might not be quite as fierce as Glasgow's Old Firm (Rangers and Celtic), it's near enough. Both clubs have suffered relegation from the **Premiership** in recent seasons (with Hearts having additionally faced administration), yet both have come roaring back to the top flight. Hibernian (aka Hibs) afforded the eastern half of the city one of its noisiest and most cathartic weekend-long celebrations in 2016, when they notched up a memorable victory over Rangers in the Scottish Cup, lifting the trophy for the first time since 1902. **Tickets** for home games are reasonably priced at around £20–30, and are normally available for sale via the clubs' respective websites.

Health

For minor ailments, pharmacists, known as **chemists** in Scotland, can dispense a limited range of drugs without a doctor's prescription. Most chemists are open standard shop hours (9am–5.30/6pm) though the "duty chemist" system obliges some to open late on a rotated basis.

In the event of an emergency, you can either turn up at the **Accident and Emergency** (A&E) department of Edinburgh's Royal Infirmary (☏ 0131 536 1000) on the southern edge of the city at 51 Little France Crescent, Old Dalkeith Road; or phone for an ambulance (☏ 999). A&E services are free to all. For non-emergency health concerns you can phone the NHS ☏ 111 service (calls are free); they can let you know the nearest place for treatment, including for dental emergencies.

Internet

Practically all accommodation in Edinburgh offers **free wi-fi** as standard and public wi-fi is widespread in cafés, public transport etc. If you don't have your own smartphone, laptop or tablet, try the cheap or free internet access provided by most public libraries.

Left luggage

There are left luggage facilities at Edinburgh Airport, East Terminal (📞 0330 223 0893; daily 4am–10pm); Glasgow Airport, Main Terminal (📞 0330 223 0893; daily 4am–9pm); Edinburgh Waverley station, Platform 19 (📞 0131 558 3829; daily 7am–11pm); Glasgow Queen Street station, near North Hannover Street entrance (📞 0141 335 3276; daily 7am–10pm); Edinburgh bus station has storage lockers (24hr); Glasgow bus station, main Concourse (no phone; daily 6am–11pm).

LGBT travellers

The Edinburgh LGBT Centre, 58a/60 Broughton St (📞 0131 556 9471) is the oldest of its kind in the UK, with a café and meeting rooms. It also organises Edinburgh's annual **Pride march** (🌐 prideedinburgh.org.uk) in mid-June, with a parade from the Scottish Parliament through the Old Town. Broughton Street, Greenside Place and Picardy Place together form the "Pink Triangle", long the locus of the Edinburgh scene, with numerous bars and clubs. 🌐 lgbtyouth.org. uk is a useful resource for younger people, while LGBT Health & Wellbeing (🌐 lgbthealth.org.uk) operate a helpline two days a week (Tues & Wed noon–9pm; 📞 0300 123 2523).

Lost Property

There are lost property units at Edinburgh Airport, East Terminal (📞 0330 223 0893; 4am–10pm) and Glasgow Airport, Main Terminal (📞 0330 223 0893; 4am–9pm). For train stations, contact Edinburgh Waverley, Platform 19 (📞 0330 024 0215; Mon–Fri 9am–5.30pm) or Glasgow Queen Street's lost property near the North Hannover

Street entrance (📞 0141 335 3276; daily 7am–10pm). For property left on buses, try Edinburgh bus station (📞 0131 555 6363) or Glasgow (📞 0141 333 3708).

Money

The basic unit of **currency** in the UK is the pound sterling (£), divided into 100 pence (p). Coins come in denominations of 1p, 2p, 5p, 10p, 20p, 50p, £1 and £2. Bank of England £5, £10, £20 and £50 banknotes are legal tender in Scotland; in addition the **Bank of Scotland (HBOS)**, the **Royal Bank of Scotland** (RBS) and the **Clydesdale Bank** issue their own banknotes in all the same denominations, plus a £100 note. At the time of going to press, £1 was worth around $1.33, €1.13, Can$1.69, Aus$1.75 and NZ$1.94. For the most up-to-date exchange rates, check the useful website 🌐 xe.com.

Credit/debit cards are by far the most convenient way to carry your money, and most hotels, shops and restaurants in Edinburgh accept the major brand cards. There are ATMs all over the city and every area has a branch of at least one of the big Scottish high-street **banks** and/or UK banks, usually with an ATM attached. General **banking hours** are Monday to Friday from 9 or 9.30am to 4 or 5pm, though some branches are open until slightly later on Thursdays. Post offices charge **no commission**, have longer opening hours, and are therefore often a good place to change money and cheques.

Opening hours

Traditional **shop hours** are Monday to Saturday 9am to 5.30 or 6pm, with many opening later on Thursdays or Fridays (around 9pm). Large supermarkets typically stay open till 8pm or 10pm and a few manage 24hr opening (excluding Sunday).

Public holidays

You'll find all banks and most offices **closed** on the following days, while everything else pretty much runs to a **Sunday schedule** (except on Christmas Day, Boxing Day, New Year's Day and January 2 when everything shuts down): Good Friday (late March/April); Easter Monday (late March/April); first and last Mondays in May; first Monday in August. Note that the second Monday in April and third Monday in September are officially public holidays in Edinburgh, though many businesses – and often public offices – remain open.

Phones

Public **payphones** are a rarity in Edinburgh, and seldom used. If you're taking your **mobile phone/cellphone** with you to Scotland, check with your service provider whether your phone will work abroad and what the call charges will be. While roaming charges were recently abolished within the EU, it's far from clear whether this will still apply to the UK if/when Britain exits the bloc. Calls to destinations further afield, however, are still unregulated and can be prohibitively expensive. Unless you have a tri-band phone, it's unlikely that a mobile bought for use in the **US** will work outside the States and vice versa. Mobiles in **Australia** and **New Zealand** generally use the same system as the UK so should work fine. Beware of premium-rate numbers, which are common for pre-recorded information services – and usually have the prefix ☏ 09.

Post

Most **post offices** are open Monday to Friday 9am–5.30pm and Saturday 9am–12.30pm, though the branch at 207a Leith Walk has some of the most comprehensive opening hours in Edinburgh (Mon–Fri 8am–8pm, Sat & Sun 8am–6pm).

Smoking

Smoking is banned in all indoor public spaces including all cafés, pubs, restaurants, clubs and public transport. These restrictions often cover e-cigarettes.

Time

Greenwich Mean Time (GMT) – equivalent to Co-ordinated Universal Time (UTC) – is used from the end of October to the end of March; for the rest of the year the country switches to **British Summer Time** (BST), one hour ahead of GMT.

Tipping

There are no fixed rules for tipping. If you think you've received good service, particularly in restaurants or cafés, you may want to leave a tip of ten percent of the total bill (unless service has already been included). It's not normal, however, to leave tips in pubs, although bar staff are sometimes offered drinks, which they may accept in the form of money.

Toilets

There's a surprisingly small number of public toilets in Edinburgh, and the figure is ever decreasing as the council sells them off. Both Waverley and Haymarket train stations, and Edinburgh bus station, have toilets, as do most department stores, free museums and galleries.

Tourist information

The official tourist board in Scotland is known as **VisitScotland** (☏ visitscotland.com) and their flagship iCentre is at 3 Princes Street, just outside Waverley Station (June 3–June 30 Mon–Sat 9am–6pm, Sun 10am–6pm; July–Sept 8 9am–7pm, Sun 10am–7pm; Sept 9–June 2 Mon–Sat 9am–5pm, Sun 10am–5pm; ☏ 0131 473 3868, ⊛ visitscotland.com/info/services/edinburgh-icentre-p234441).

As well as reserving accommodation, you can book tours, buy tickets for sights (including multi-passes) and transport (including ferries if you're planning on heading on to the Highlands and islands). For listings magazines and websites, *The List* (magazine every two months; ⊛ list.co.uk) and *The Skinny* (magazine bi-monthly; ⊛ theskinny.co.uk) are both excellent and invaluable sources of upcoming events in Edinburgh and in-depth cultural analysis, particularly during the Festival when they ramp up coverage.

Travellers with disabilities

Edinburgh is an old city; installing ramps, lifts, wide doorways and disabled toilets is, unfortunately, impossible in many of the city's older and historic buildings. Access has improved, however, with some of the city's most iconic attractions – including Edinburgh Castle (see page 28), the Palace of Holyrood House (see page 58) and the Scottish Parliament (see page 59) – relatively accessible. Some hotels and a handful of B&Bs have one or two adapted rooms, usually on the ground floor and with step-free showers, grab rails and wider doorways.

Most **trains** in Scotland have wheelchair lifts, and assistance is, in theory, available at all manned stations – see ⊛ scotrail.co.uk/plan-your-journey/accessible-travel. Wheelchair-users (alone or with a companion) and blind or partially sighted people (with a companion only) are automatically given thirty to fifty percent reductions on train fares. For more information and advice contact the disability charity Capability Scotland (☏ 0131 313 5510, ⊛ capability-scotland.org.uk).

Travelling with children

Edinburgh is a great place for children and needn't necessarily put parents under undue financial strain, especially if they make use of the city's numerous parks and gardens. Public transport is free for under-6s and all major museums and galleries can be visited free of charge. Kids are generally welcomed in cafés and restaurants, but less so in pubs where there's usually a child policy notice at the entrance.

Historic Environment Scotland and National Trust for Scotland

Many of Scotland's most treasured sights come under the control of the privately run National Trust for Scotland (⊛ nts.org.uk) or the state-run Historic Environment Scotland (⊛ historicenvironment.scot); we've quoted "NTS" or "HES" respectively for each site reviewed in this Guide. Both organizations charge an admission fee for most places, and these can be quite high.

If you think you'll be visiting more than half a dozen NTS properties, or more than a dozen HES ones, it's worth taking annual membership, which costs around £47.25 (HES) or £48 (NTS), and allows free admission to their properties. In addition, both the NTS and HES offer short-term passes (NTS £26.50/3 days, £31.50/7 days; HES £31/3 days out of 5; £42/7 days out of 14).

Festivals and events

Edinburgh International Science Festival

first fortnight in April ⓦ www.science festival.co.uk

The first event of its kind in the world, this educational survey of everything from digital animation and immersive virtual reality to primates and human evolution has gone from strength to strength over the last two decades. Perfect for children, families and rainy days. Venues all over the city, including the National Museum of Scotland (see page 50), Summerhall (see page 119), Royal Botanic Garden (see page 94) and Edinburgh Zoo (see page 106). Some events free; some ticketed (£5-15).

Beltane Fire Festival

April 30 ⓦ beltane.org

Forget dancing round the Maypole – each spring, Edinburgh's Calton Hill banishes winter and sees in summer in a riot of flame, drumming and body paint with this contemporary interpretation of an ancient Celtic ritual. From informal and fairly anarchic beginnings in the late 80s, Beltane has grown to become one of the highlights of Edinburgh's festival calendar. The febrile, hedonistic atmosphere and outlandish theatre of it all never fail to impress, while the incongruous semi-splendour of the National Monument setting only adds to the spectacle. Fans of *Lord of the Rings*, *Game of Thrones* et al will lap this up. Unmissable. Tickets £10.

Hidden Door Festival

end of May/early June

ⓦ hiddendoorblog.org

Probably Edinburgh's hippest and most creative new(ish) festival, Hidden Door is a not-for-profit celebration of the cutting edge and experimental, covering music, art, theatre, film and spoken word over ten days in late May and early June. Recent guests have included the likes of Anna Meredith, Gazelle Twin and Riot Jazz Brass Band, as well as Edinburgh's own former Makar, Ron Butlin and Leith's veteran stage hard man Tam Dean Burn. Dedicated to seeking out parts of the city other festivals can't reach, the 2017 event breathed life back into the faded art deco splendour of the old Leith Theatre, the first time the place had opened its doors to the public in 28 years. Free noon–6pm; ticketed 6pm–late (generally £10–20).

Edinburgh International Film Festival

June 20/21 to July 1/2 ⓦ edfilmfest.org.uk

Seventy years young, this is the world's longest continually running film festival, feted by everyone from Mark Kermode to Martin Scorsese and – over the years – home to UK premieres of *Annie Hall*, *Taxi Driver* and *Blade Runner* to name a few. Expect a dazzling and comprehensive programme of domestic and foreign features new and old, world premieres, documentary, shorts, themed retrospectives, archival screenings and big-name Q&As. Based at the Filmhouse (see page 91), with some screenings in other cinemas. Tickets generally around £10–15.

Edinburgh Jazz & Blues Festival

third week in July

ⓦ edinburghjazzfestival.com

Now the largest festival of its kind in Britain, hosting everyone from the Bad Plus and Ibibio Sound Machine to BB King and Dizzy Gillespie, this caters to most strands of jazz, blues and beyond. Long highlights of Edinburgh's packed summer calendar are the inaugural

Mardi Gras held in the Grassmarket on the opening Sat, and the Carnival parade and al fresco performances in Princes Street Gardens on Sun; both events are free. Gigs all over the city including Festival Theatre (see page 56), Traverse Theatre (see page 91) and George Square. Tickets generally £10–25 (see website for student special offers). Cash only at smaller venues like the *The Jazz Bar* (see page 57).

Edinburgh Art Festival

late July to late August ⓦ edinburghart
festival.com, ⓦ nationalgalleries.org/tickets
The UK's largest visual arts festival, with high-profile exhibitions by the likes of Tracey Emin, Douglas Gordon and Ron Mueck, as well as retrospectives of everyone from Robert Mapplethorpe to John Bellany. Virtually every gallery in the city participates and new work is also commissioned each year by emerging native talent. Most exhibitions free; National Galleries' exhibitions £10–12.

Edinburgh International Festival

early to late August ⓦ eif.co.uk
The original Edinburgh Festival, sometimes called the "Official Festival", was conceived in 1947 when, after decades of war, poverty and racism, a handful of wise civic leaders sought to embrace cultural diversity and "provide a platform for the flowering of the human spirit". Initially dominated by opera, other elements such as theatre, ballet, dance and classical music were gradually introduced, and it's still very much a highbrow event. That said, the festival has widened its high-cultural horizons in recent years, with PJ Harvey, Mogwai and a Joe Boyd-directed Incredible String Band tribute all making it on to the programme. Performances take place at the city's larger venues such as the Usher Hall (see page 91)

and the Festival Theatre (see page 56). Tickets £10–95.

Royal Edinburgh Military Tattoo

early to late August ⓦ edintattoo.co.uk
Staged nightly in the spectacular stadium of the Edinburgh Castle Esplanade, the Military Tattoo is an unashamed display of pomp and military circumstance, and one of the most expensive seats of all the capital's events. The programme of choreographed drills, massed pipe bands and pyrotechnics has been a feature of the Edinburgh Festival for over half a century, attracting an incredible fourteen million people. Tickets (£25–300 depending on seat location and day, plus a £5 booking fee if bought online) need to be booked well in advance. Look out for cheap preview tickets in early August – keep an eye on the website.

Edinburgh International Book Festival

last two weeks of August
ⓦ edbookfest.co.uk
The world's largest celebration of the written word is held in a tented village in Charlotte Square (recently expanding into George St) in the thick of Edinburgh's August arts frenzy. It offers talks, readings and signings by a star-studded line-up of visiting authors, as well as panel discussions and workshops. Well-known Scottish authors such as Ron Butlin, John Burnside, Alexander McCall-Smith and Ian Rankin (most recently in conversation with arch provocateur, Cosi Fanni Tutti) are good for an appearance most years, while the 2017 Outriders project included novelist Kevin McNeil tracing the links between Jorge Luis Borges and Robert Louis Stevenson. Visitors from a bit further afield have included Paul Auster, Marina Warner and George Monbiot. Tickets generally £10–15.

FESTIVALS AND EVENTS

Edinburgh Festivals and Festival Venues

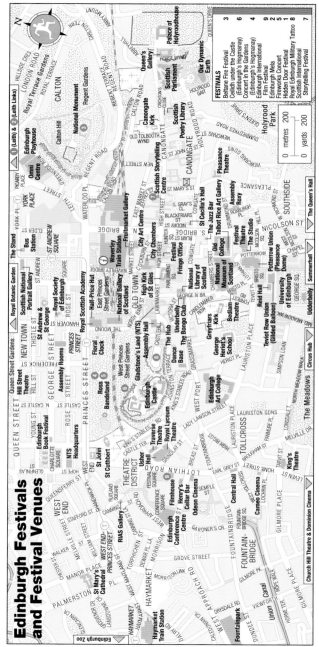

FESTIVALS

Beltane Fire Festival	3
Ceilidh under the Castle (Edinburgh's Hogmanay)	6
Concert in the Gardens (Edinburgh's Hogmanay)	4
Edinburgh International Film Festival	9
Edinburgh Mela	2
Fireworks Concert	5
Hidden Door Festival	1
Royal Edinburgh Military Tattoo	8
Scottish International Storytelling Festival	7

0 metres 200
0 yards 200

Fireworks Concert

late August ⓦ eif.co.uk

Based in Princes Street Gardens but visible from all over the city, this is the pyrotechnical culmination of the International Festival, with hundreds of thousands of fireworks making it one of the biggest (and noisiest) of its kind in the world. Tickets (£13.50 standing, £32 seated) sell out well in advance. The concert begins on the last day of the festival at 9/9.30pm.

Edinburgh Mela

late August/early September

ⓦ edinburgh-mela.co.uk

Edinburgh's very own take on WOMAD, this is Scotland's biggest world music and dance festival with performances, cross-cultural collaborations, workshops and ethnic food stalls amid the green spaces of Leith Links. Recent commissioned works include a high profile 2015 link-up with the Military Tattoo (see page 145), featuring a cast of Bollywood professionals and local dancers. Tickets £5.

Scottish International Storytelling Festival

late October ⓦ tracscotland.org/festivals/ scottish-international-storytelling-festivalif. co.uk

Based in the Royal Mile's Scottish Storytelling Centre (see page 36), this much loved, family-friendly festival draws its inspiration from Scotland's myriad oral traditions, hosting storytellers and musicians from around the world over ten days in October. Some events free; tickets £6–15.

Edinburgh's Hogmanay

When hard line Presbyterian clerics in the sixteenth century **abolished Christmas** for being a Catholic mass, the Scots instead put their energy into greeting the New Year, or **Hogmanay**. While the old tradition of "**first-footing**" – visiting neighbours and bearing gifts – is dying out across Scotland, Edinburgh has once again captured the world's imagination with its famous **street party** (ⓦ edinburghshogmanay.com). Originally a free – and freely inebriated – local gathering in the Royal Mile, it has, like most of the capital's festivals, latterly taken on a life of its own, with the focus now on Princes Street and ticket numbers restricted to 60, 000 ever since the legendary 1996–97 event clocked in at almost half a million revellers. Regularly cited by travel experts and bucket listers as one of the globe's must-experience events, the party has grown from a drunken, stranger-snogging celebration of the midnight bells to a recently revamped, six-hour marathon including the **Ceilidh under the Castle**; the **Concert in the Gardens** featuring A-list **pop, rock and indie bands**; flash mobs and fire eaters; and pyrotechnics that'd put Handel to shame. There's also a side programme including a **Torchlight Procession** down the Royal Mile towards Holyrood Park (Dec 30), a **Bairns Afore** afternoon celebration for children and families (Dec 31), and the infamous **Loony Dook** on New Year's Day, wherein often still-drunk tourists and locals enter the frigid waters of the Forth. **Ticket** details for all events are available on the website, though the street party (£26) often sells out well in advance, as does the Ceilidh under the Castle (£52.50) and the Concert in the Gardens (£60); note that a ticket for the latter also allows wristband access from Princes Street Gardens to the street party, but not vice versa.

The Fringe

"Welcome to the Alliance of Defiance". So ran the headline on the **Edinburgh Festival Fringe** website (Ⓦ edfringe.com) during their 70th anniversary year in 2017. Seven decades earlier eight theatre companies had turned up uninvited to the Edinburgh International Festival (see page 145) and were refused entry; undaunted they proceeded to perform their shows in alternative venues on what critics and commentators dubbed "the fringe" of the official festival. The idea caught on: now indisputably the "largest platform on earth for creative freedom", the Fringe sees over **fifty thousand performances** of over **three thousand shows**, in almost **three hundred venues**, with performers – and audiences – hailing from every corner of the globe. While the headlining names at the International Festival reinforce its cultural credibility, it is the dynamism, spontaneity and sheer exuberance of the Fringe that dominate Edinburgh every August, giving the city its unique atmosphere and doubling its population. These days, the most prominent and ubiquitous aspect of the Fringe is **comedy**, having overtaken theatre as the largest genre in 2008. As well as sell-out audiences and quotable reviews, most of the comedy acts are chasing an **Edinburgh Comedy Award**, given to the outstanding stand-up or comedy cabaret. At the same time, the Fringe's **theatre** programme shows no signs of dying out, with hundreds of brand-new cutting edge and often controversial works airing alongside offbeat classics and familiar Shakespearean tragedies. The **venues** are often as imaginative as the shows themselves: play-parks, restaurants and even parked cars have all been used to stage plays. The Fringe also offers fine musicals, dance, children's shows, exhibitions, lectures and music; in fact every facet of human expression is usually covered somewhere or other amidst the chaotic, sprawling arts labyrinth that is central Edinburgh in August. The whole thing kicks off and winds up on the same days as the International Festival, and usually runs for just over three weeks.

Tickets

Ticket prices for most Fringe shows start around £6, and average from £10 to £15 at the main venues, with the best-known acts going for even more, though there are often cheap preview deals on the opening weekend and always deals at the Half Price Hut (see below). Tickets are sold at the Fringe Box Office (see below), as well as online or at venues. Performances are staged around the clock, with most scheduled to run for an hour.

FESTIVAL FRINGE BOX OFFICE

MAP P.30, POCKET MAP C15
180 High St ☎ 0131 226 0026, Ⓦ edfringe.com. Box office June 7–June 11 & July 17–July 30 daily 10am–6pm; June 12–July 16 Mon–Sat noon–3pm; July 31–Aug 28 daily 9am–9pm; phone bookings June 7–June 11 & July 17–July 30 daily 10am–6pm; June 12–July 16 Mon–Sat 10am–6pm; July 31–Aug 28 daily 9am–9pm.

Although some shows are bookable via the website earlier in the year, the box office at the Fringe HQ in the Royal Mile generally opens from early June onwards, upon publication of the full Fringe programme, with tickets available for sale in person, online, by telephone or via the downloadable app.

HALF PRICE HUT
Map p.68, Pocket map B14
Mound Precinct, by the National Gallery of Scotland ⓦ tickets.edfringe.com/box-office/virgin-money-half-price-hut. During the festival daily 10am–9pm.
This is the place to head for bargains, with discounted tickets for Fringe shows struggling to woo audiences. Note that tickets are available for shows happening on the day you buy them and the following morning only, and can likewise only be purchased in person.

Venues

Most of the venue spaces across the city are colonized by the four dominant Fringe companies – Assembly, Pleasance, Gilded Balloon and Underbelly, all safe bets for decent shows and a bit of star-spotting.

ASSEMBLY ROXY/ASSEMBLY ROOMS
Roxy 2 Roxburgh Place ☎ 0131 623 3001, ⓦ assemblyroxy.com; Rooms 54 George St ☎ 0131 623 3030.
Longest running of the multi-venue operators, providing a grand George St setting for top-of-the-range drama and big-name music and comedy acts, and more intimate spaces at the Roxy.

GILDED BALLOON
Teviot Row House, Bristo Square, Southside ☎ 0131 622 6555, ⓦ gildedballoon.co.uk.
The most elegant of the main Old Town venues. It's predominantly mainstream comedy here, although they don't shy away from championing emerging talent.

PLEASANCE COURTYARD/PLEASANCE DOME
Courtyard 60 The Pleasance, Old Town; Dome Potterrow, Bristo Square, Southside ☎ 0131 556 6550, ⓦ pleasance.co.uk.
The Pleasance courtyard beer garden is a legendary Fringe hangout. Indoors you'll find offbeat comedy mixing with whimsical appearances by Radio 4 panellists. The Dome is located in one of Edinburgh University's student unions, with auditoria accessed from the sky-lit dome room.

THE UNDERBELLY
Bristo Square, Southside ☎ 0844 545 8252, ⓦ underbelly.co.uk.
Underbelly's giant, inflatable upside-down cow – the Udderbelly – is one of the Fringe's most outlandish venues, accompanied by plenty of al fresco drinking "pasture" in George Square Gardens.

Chronology

c.142AD Romans establish a fort at Cramond, in the domain of the Celtic Votadini tribe.

c.400–700 The Gododdin – descendants of the Votadini – establish hillfort of Din Eidyn on Castle Rock.

c.638 Din Eidyn falls to the Kingdom of Northumbria and assumes the Old English suffix, "-burh".

c.973 Lothian formally granted to Kenneth II by English king Edgar the Peaceful.

c.1130 King David 1 grants Edinburgh royal burgh status.

1291–1314 Edinburgh falls into English hands during the first of the Wars of Scottish Independence.

1320 The Declaration of Arbroath, asserting Scottish independence, is sent to the Pope.

1329 Robert The Bruce grants Edinburgh a new charter with jurisdiction over the port of Leith, allowing the city to prosper from foreign trade and establish itself as Scotland's permanent capital.

c.1365 Low Countries-born chronicler Froissart describes Edinburgh as "the Paris of Scotland".

c.1513 Work begins on Edinburgh's defensive Flodden Wall after the Scots are defeated by the English at the Battle of Flodden Field.

c.1544 Edinburgh is sacked and burned by the forces of Henry VIII after Scotland resists his attempt to marry off his son to Mary, Queen of Scots.

1560 Siege of Leith by English troops in alliance with Scottish Protestants ends in the Treaty of Edinburgh, the dissolution of Scotland's long-standing mutual defence pact with France (aka the Auld Alliance) and the establishment of Protestantism as Scotland's official religion.

1561 Mary, Queen of Scots lands in Leith after thirteen years in French exile, entering a cauldron of religious and political turmoil.

1567 Mary is forced to abdicate after a disastrous reign at Holyrood Palace, including the infamous murders of her secretary David Rizzio and consort Lord Darnley, with Reformation leader John Knox calling for her execution.

1603 Mary's son and heir James VI of Scotland becomes James I of England and Ireland with the Union of the Crowns.

1650 Edinburgh is occupied by English Puritan Oliver Cromwell after the Battle of Dunbar.

1651 English Parliament passes the Tender of Union, effectively annexing Scotland and dissolving the Scottish Parliament in Edinburgh.

1661 Re-institution of the Scottish Parliament following the restoration of Charles II.

1689 Scottish Parliament passes the Claim of Right act, asserting Charles' son, James VII's forfeiture of the Scottish throne and paving the way for a Presbyterian Church of Scotland.

1707 The Scottish Parliament is dissolved as Scotland signs the Act of Union with England, partly in response to the 1705 Alien Act, which had rendered Scots in England as foreign nationals, and placed an embargo on Scottish imports into English colonies; English spy Daniel Defoe reports on the violent and overwhelming opposition to the union.

1745 James VII's grandson Charles Edward Stuart aka Bonnie Prince Charlie, enters Edinburgh to cheering crowds and occupies Holyrood Palace for over a month, proclaiming "....the pretended Union of these Kingdoms being now at an end".

1746 Stuart dynasty meets final defeat at Battle of Culloden.

Late 1740s–c.1800 Edinburgh gains international renown as the centre of the Scottish Enlightenment, led by such revered thinkers as David Hume and Adam Smith.

1767 Work begins on the Georgian New Town as Edinburgh outgrows its medieval boundaries.

1867 Edinburgh City Improvement Act sees work commence on clearing Old Town slums.

1947 Edinburgh hosts its first International Festival.

1996 Danny Boyle's hugely acclaimed film adaptation of the Irvine Welsh novel, *Trainspotting*, affords Edinburgh a youthful international cachet, accelerating its transformation into – and reclaiming its place as – one of the most dynamic, cosmopolitan and desirable cities in Europe.

1999 Scottish Devolution sees the reopening of the Scottish Parliament.

2008 The global financial crash and UK government bail-out of Royal Bank of Scotland dents Edinburgh's burgeoning financial sector and its rampant housing market.

2011 The Scottish National Party win a majority at Holyrood and call a referendum on independence to be held in 2014.

2014 The No side wins 55 to 45 in the independence referendum.

2016 In the EU membership referendum Scotland votes to remain 62 to 38, while the UK as a whole votes to leave.

2017 Scottish and Welsh governments consistently excluded from Brexit negotiations; both reject the UK government's great repeal bill as a Westminster power grab.

SMALL PRINT

Publishing informa

First edition 2018

Distribution
UK, Ireland and Europe
Apa Publications (UK) Ltd; sales@roughguides.com
United States and Canada
Ingram Publisher Services; ips@ingramcontent.com
Australia and New Zealand
Woodslane; info@woodslane.com.au
Southeast Asia
Apa Publications (SN) Pte; sales@roughguides.com
Worldwide
Apa Publications (UK) Ltd; sales@roughguides.com
Special Sales, Content Licensing and CoPublishing
Rough Guides can be purchased in bulk quantities at discounted prices. We can
create special editions, personalised jackets and corporate imprints tailored to
your needs. sales@roughguides.com.
roughguides.com
Printed in China by RR Donnelley Asia Printing Solutions Limited
A catalogue record for this book is available from the British Library
The publishers and authors have done their best to ensure the accuracy and
currency of all the information in **Pocket Rough Guide Edinburgh**, however, they
can accept no responsibility for any loss, injury, or inconvenience sustained by
any traveller as a result of information or advice contained in the guide.

Rough Guide credits

Editor: Neil McQuillian
Cartography: Ed Wright
Managing editor: Rachel Lawrence
Picture editor: Aude Vauconsant
Cover photo research: Mark Thomas

Original design: Richard Czapnik
Senior DTP coordinator: Dan May
Head of DTP and Pre-Press:
Rebeka Davies

Author: Brendon Griffin has lived in Edinburgh, on and off, for much of his adult
life. When not wandering around Arthur's Seat, he writes and edits for Rough
Guides, tinkers with interior design, reviews Latin, African and Brazilian music
and plays percussion (badly).

Help us update

We've gone to a lot of effort to ensure that the first edition of the **Pocket Rough Guide Edinburgh** is accurate and up-to-date. However, things change – places get "discovered", opening hours are notoriously fickle, restaurants and rooms raise prices or lower standards. If you feel we've got it wrong or left something out, we'd like to know, and if you can remember the address, the price, the hours, the phone number, so much the better.

Please send your comments with the subject line "**Pocket Rough Guide Edinburgh Update**" to mail@uk.roughguides.com. We'll credit all contributions and send a copy of the next edition (or any other Rough Guide if you prefer) for the very best emails.

Photo Credits

(Key: T-top; C-centre; B-bottom; L-left; R-right)

Alamy 8, 16B, 17B, 20C, 21B, 22T, 24C, 25T, 53, 64, 65, 68, 74, 82, 83, 85, 90, 96, 98, 102, 103, 105, 111, 112, 114, 118

Alan Donaldson/Norn 22B, 104

David Bann 43

Douglas Macgilvray/Apa Publications 13B, 20C, 20B, 40, 46, 59, 75, 88, 120, 124

Dr Neil's Garden Trust 14/15T

Edinburgh Printmakers 81

Getty Images 6, 12, 13T, 14/15B, 22C, 23C, 25C, 36, 38, 44, 55, 56, 77, 97, 110, 121, 128/129

Harmonium 5

iStock 1, 2T, 14B, 15C, 16T,17T, 18/19T, 24T, 24B, 28, 35, 60, 62, 63, 71, 72, 73, 87, 92, 106, 109, 115, 116, 117, 123, 126, 127

Karol Kozlowski/AWL Images 2BL, 2CR

Keith Inglis/Monteiths 42

L'Escargot Bleu 84

Picfair 4, 94, 101, 119

Rhian McIntosh/The Caley Sample Room 113

Shutterstock 2BR, 18B, 19B, 21T 21C, 23T, 23B, 25B, 26/27, 31, 32, 33, 39, 41, 50, 66, 67, 70, 76, 86, 95, 100, 107, 108, 125, 134/135

Cover Edinburgh castle **Maurizio Rellini/4Corners**

Index